YOU ARE SOLD!

How to Create Deals Customers Can't Refuse

By

Rohit Soni

Published by Zorba Books, October 2024
Website: www.zorbabooks.com
Email: info@zorbabooks.com
Author Name: Rohit Soni

Title: YOU ARE SOLD!

Printbook ISBN: 978-93-5896-247-5
Ebook ISBN: 978-93-5896-727-2

Zorba Books Pvt. Ltd. (opc)
Sushant Arcade,
Next to Courtyard Marriot,
Sushant Lok 1, Gurgaon – 122009, India

TABLE OF CONTENTS

INTRODUCTION

I am a 24 year old Marketer who started my journey at just 17, at that time Digital Marketing was just getting started. People were interested in it, but no one knew what was upon us.

At that time I thought to myself just one thing, what if I make money online?

I see Youtubers do it, I see newbies course sellers do it, it was at that moment I said "Let me look into some skills and one of the biggest skills that stood out to me was "Copywriting". When I first heard about it, I said "ohh Man are people even making money by writing for other people?"

The answer was YES, so I took some courses and started getting into it. I started pitching it to people, **0 Clients** for 7 months. It wasn't until COVID that I signed my first client. Here's something I wanted to tell you: it's never over until it's over because the moment I signed my first client I got 3 referrals from the same person that month and in a matter of 7 days, Now I am working with 4 clients!

That's the power of getting results, creating amazing offers and stepping up your game in the online world.

This Book will act as a lifetime guide for you on how to create offers people cannot refuse because if you get good at it, You can help your clients generate revenue anywhere and at any time.

FOREWORD

I met Rohit for the first time on Zoom virtually, back in April 2021, usually I don't give my time to just anyone but he offered me something I couldn't deny.

Simply on facebook he sent me a message saying "I would love to work with you for free for 7 days and get your calls booked with potential clients" who would refuse to that? But it was just the beginning for me to know how talented and dedicated he was. I said yes, why not.

When I first met him, I immediately told him "Rohit if I am going to work with you I want you to know one thing about me, Either I trust you or I don't there's no middle way here with me." Here I am super proud to share with you he is a sincere dedicated man who loves to do marketing, give results to his clients and take care of almost everything needed.

My experience with him over the last 4 years has been nothing short of spectacular.

I have seen increased income, increased profits, increased happiness and joy in my life through the campaigns he has created for me.

From a business perspective I can tell you this book is one of the best investments you can make if you're a marketer, business owner, freelancer, entrepreneur or sales professional.

Rohit has taken everything he has learned and packaged it in a way that you should be reading it and immediately implementing the same in your business. So to anyone reading this I highly recommend you take action to see lasting results because Rohit's offers are irresistible.

– Ken D Foster
Business Coach, Best-Selling Author, Media Advisor

ABOUT THE AUTHOR

Rohit Soni is a trailblazer in the world of marketing. He is an Author of 2 books, 2 times TEDx Speaker & runs his own Marketing Media company called Amplify Media which is widely famous for helping world class coaches scale their business from 6 to 7 to even 8 figures.

He has worked with the likes of Terrance Mchanon, Ken D Foster & Jackie Woodside

His expertise has made him one of the best Marketers in the world.

Apart from that Rohit Soni also has a podcast called "Rohit Soni Leadership Podcast" with over 85+ episodes where he interviews people and share their success stories.

Laptop lifestyle is something that Rohit Soni enjoys he has a mission to guide people in India to learn high income skills & start a business from anywhere like he did it for himself.

INTRODUCTION: THE POWER OF AN IRRESISTIBLE OFFER

In today's overcrowded marketplace, attention is currency. If you can't get people's attention, you're dead in the water. The secret? Creating an offer that is so compelling, your prospect can't say no.

It's simple. But simple isn't easy. So, how do you create offers that turn the sceptical "I'm just looking" types into committed buyers? That's what this book is about.

Dan Kennedy, one of the most influential direct response marketers, said it best:

"If you can get someone to say 'that would be stupid for me not to buy,' then you've won the marketing game."

By the end of this book, you'll be equipped with the tools to make every offer you present one that people can't resist—one that demands action.

Chapter 1

WHAT MAKES AN OFFER IRRESISTIBLE?

What Makes an Offer Irresistible?

Introduction

In today's fast-paced, competitive marketplace, the key to standing out is making your offer irresistible. It's not just about having a good product or service; it's about crafting an offer that compels people to take action immediately. When done right, an irresistible offer feels like a no-brainer to potential customers—a deal so good they can't afford to pass it up. But what exactly makes an offer irresistible? It's a blend of psychology, value perception, urgency, and trust. In this chapter, we'll explore these elements in detail and uncover the strategies businesses and marketers can use to create offers that not only attract attention but also convert consistently.

1: Understanding the Psychology Behind Offers

At its core, the success of any offer is deeply rooted in psychology. Human behavior is driven by a series of innate motivators—whether it's the fear of missing out (FOMO), the allure of gaining something valuable, or the desire to make life easier or more enjoyable. To make an offer irresistible, businesses must tap into these psychological triggers.

Fear of Missing Out (FOMO)

FOMO is a powerful psychological driver. When consumers believe they might miss out on an exclusive opportunity, their urgency to act increases. Limited-time offers or limited-quantity products play on this fear, making the consumer feel that if they don't act now, they may never get the chance again. Consider flash sales or exclusive pre-orders—these strategies leverage FOMO to great effect. For an offer to tap into this successfully, it must create a genuine sense of scarcity or urgency.

Reciprocity

Reciprocity is another fundamental psychological principle that makes offers more appealing. When someone gives you something, you feel a subconscious obligation to give back. In marketing, this can be achieved by offering a freebie, discount, or valuable information upfront. For example, providing a free trial or a no-cost consultation before asking for a sale can create a sense of reciprocity, making the prospect more likely to say "yes" to your offer in return.

Social Proof

Humans are social creatures, and we often look to others when making decisions. This is why social proof, such as testimonials, reviews, or endorsements, can significantly enhance an offer's appeal. When consumers see others who have benefited from a product or service, they feel more confident that they too will experience similar positive results. To make an offer irresistible, providing clear, credible, and compelling social proof can be a game-changer.

2: Crafting Value Perception: More Than Just Discounts

Creating an irresistible offer is not just about slashing prices. While discounts can certainly make an offer tempting, value perception is far more complex and multifaceted. It's about making the customer feel that they are getting more than they are paying for—not just in terms of cost but in terms of the problem it solves, the benefits it delivers, and the emotional satisfaction it provides.

Positioning the Offer as a Solution

One of the most effective ways to make an offer irresistible is to position it as a solution to a pressing problem. People are more likely to purchase if they believe the product or service will solve an issue they care about or improve their lives in some meaningful way. For example, if you're selling a time management tool, it's not just about promoting the features of the product but rather focusing on the time it will save your customers and how much more productive they will feel.

Added Bonuses and Perceived Value

Another strategy to enhance value perception is to offer added bonuses that complement the main offer. These bonuses should align with the core product or service, increasing its usefulness or making the experience more complete. For example, a company selling online courses might add free templates, checklists, or access to a community group as a bonus. These extras increase the perceived value without significantly increasing the cost of providing the offer.

Price Anchoring

Price anchoring is a powerful tool in shaping value perception. This technique involves showing a higher original price before presenting the discounted offer, making the new price seem like an incredible deal in comparison. For instance, if you're offering a product for $50 but it was previously priced at $100, the customer feels like they're getting a significant bargain. Even though the $50 price might be your standard rate, the perception of saving 50% makes the offer much more attractive.

3: Creating Urgency and Scarcity

Urgency and scarcity are two pillars of an irresistible offer. Without a reason to act now, many potential customers will procrastinate and eventually forget about the offer altogether. Crafting a sense of urgency and scarcity nudges them to make a decision more quickly.

Limited-Time Offers

One of the most common ways to create urgency is through limited-time offers. These offers have an expiration date, making it clear that customers must act quickly to take advantage. Whether it's a sale that ends in 24 hours, a discount code that expires at midnight, or a time-sensitive bonus, the ticking clock pushes people to act faster than they would otherwise.

Exclusive Availability

Exclusivity plays a key role in scarcity. When an offer is made available to only a select group of people, it increases its perceived value. This could be through member-only discounts, early access to a product launch, or a VIP package. People are naturally drawn to what they can't easily get, and by limiting access, you make your offer more desirable.

Limited Quantities

Another scarcity tactic is to limit the quantity of the offer. For example, letting customers know that "only 100 units are available" or "only 5 seats remain" adds pressure to act quickly. This scarcity taps into the fear of missing out and can significantly increase conversions. However, it's essential that the scarcity is real—false scarcity can backfire and damage trust in your brand.

4: Building Trust and Credibility

Even the most compelling offer will fail if your audience doesn't trust you. Trust is the foundation

To craft an irresistible offer, you first need to understand the core components:

1. **Clear Value Proposition:** The offer must clearly communicate what the customer is getting and why it's a must-have.

   Example: When Domino's Pizza first launched, their offer wasn't "we make great pizza." It was "30 minutes or less, or it's free." The value was in the speed, not necessarily the pizza itself.
2. **Perceived Value:** The customer must believe that they are getting more than what they're paying for.

   Example: McDonald's created the Happy Meal—an ordinary meal packaged with a toy. Kids want it not for the burger but for the toy, which dramatically increases the perceived value.
3. **Specificity:** Vague offers don't sell. Specific offers do. A claim of "we'll help you lose weight fast" is weak compared to "lose 10 pounds in 30 days or your money back."
4. **Scarcity:** People want what they can't have. Limiting the availability of your offer makes it more desirable.

   Example: Think of concert tickets or limited-time Black Friday deals. People are driven by the fear of missing out.
5. **Risk Reversal:** One of the biggest hurdles for a prospect is the fear of making a mistake. Remove the risk, and you'll open the floodgates.

   Example: Zappos.com built their empire by offering free shipping and returns. They knew that if they removed the risk, people would buy more—and they did.

Quote: "An offer with no risk is like a no-brainer. It eliminates all objections and friction from the buying decision." – Rohit Soni

Chapter 2

UNDERSTANDING YOUR AUDIENCE'S CORE DESIRES

Understanding your audience's core desires is essential for creating effective content, products, or services that resonate deeply with your target market. Whether you're a marketer, business owner, or content creator, getting to the heart of what motivates your audience can transform the way you connect with them. This chapter explores the psychology behind audience desires, how to uncover them, and how to use this knowledge to build meaningful relationships with your customers.

1: The Psychology of Desires

At the root of all human behavior is desire. Whether consciously or subconsciously, people make decisions based on fulfilling certain needs or desires. According to psychologist Abraham Maslow, human needs can be organized into a hierarchy, starting with basic physiological needs and moving up to more complex desires like self-actualization. Understanding this hierarchy is essential to understanding why people act the way they do and what drives them to make specific decisions.

Maslow's Hierarchy of Needs consists of five levels:

1. **Physiological needs** – basic survival needs like food, water, and shelter.
2. **Safety needs** – security, health, and stability.
3. **Social needs** – love, friendship, and belonging.
4. **Esteem needs** – respect, recognition, and status.
5. **Self-actualization** – personal growth, self-improvement, and the pursuit of fulfilling potential.

Each level represents a deeper layer of human motivation. While many marketers and businesses focus on more surface-level desires, understanding where your audience is on this hierarchy can provide you with a more profound connection. Are they seeking security in an unstable world, or are they trying to improve themselves and fulfill their potential? Knowing which desire is at the forefront can help shape your messaging to meet those needs directly.

But beyond Maslow, other psychological principles influence consumer behavior, such as the desire for instant gratification, the need for social validation, or the fear of missing out (FOMO). Recognizing these forces can provide insights into how your audience interacts with products, services, and content.

Key Takeaway:

The core desires of your audience are not just wants—they are deep-rooted psychological needs. Whether it's a need for belonging, safety, or self-actualization, uncovering which desire drives your audience can unlock more meaningful engagement and loyalty.

2: Identifying Your Audience's Core Desires

Identifying your audience's core desires requires both research and intuition. No two audiences are the same, and their desires may vary depending on demographics, psychographics, and situational factors. To uncover these desires, you'll need a combination of qualitative and quantitative research.

Step 1: Build Customer Personas

Customer personas are fictional representations of your ideal customers. They help you visualize who you're targeting and what motivates them. Creating a persona involves gathering data on demographics (age, gender, income, etc.), psychographics (values, interests, behaviors), and behaviors related to your product or service.

Ask yourself:

- What is their age range?
- What is their occupation?
- What are their daily challenges?
- What keeps them up at night?
- What are their goals, and how can your product or service help them achieve those goals?

Step 2: Engage in Direct Conversations

Direct interaction with your audience is one of the most effective ways to understand their core desires. Surveys, interviews, and focus groups can provide invaluable insights into what your audience truly wants. Rather than assuming, asking them directly about their motivations can uncover desires you might not have considered.

Questions you might ask include:

- What are your biggest pain points?
- What would make your life easier?
- What are your aspirations, both personally and professionally?
- What would success look like to you?

By listening to the language they use, you can better understand not only their explicit desires but also their emotional drivers.

Step 3: Analyze Behavior Data

While direct conversations are crucial, analyzing behavior can provide a different kind of insight. Look at data from website analytics, social media engagement, and purchasing patterns. For instance, which blog posts get the most engagement? Which products sell the fastest? These patterns can reveal what your audience is gravitating towards and what desires they may be trying to fulfill.

Step 4: Study Competitors and Trends

Look at what your competitors are doing well and how their audience is responding. This can provide clues into what resonates with your shared audience. Additionally, keeping up with industry trends and social movements can help you understand how external factors might be shaping your audience's desires. For example, sustainability has become a core desire for many consumers in recent years due to growing environmental concerns.

Key Takeaway:

To effectively meet your audience's desires, you need a multifaceted approach—building personas, engaging in direct conversations, analyzing behavioral data, and studying industry trends. The more data you gather, the clearer the picture of their core desires will become.

3: Leveraging Desires in Content Creation

Once you've identified your audience's desires, the next step is to leverage that understanding in your content creation. Whether you're writing blog posts, producing videos, or crafting social media content, aligning your messaging with your audience's core desires can increase engagement and loyalty.

Tailoring Content to Emotional Drivers

Every piece of content should connect with your audience emotionally. By focusing on their desires, you're not just delivering information; you're providing a solution to a problem or fulfilling a need. For instance, if your audience craves a sense of belonging, your content can focus on building a community. If they are driven by self-improvement, your content can offer tips for personal growth or career development.

Examples of Desire-Based Content:

1. **Desire for Status**: Highlight testimonials, success stories, and case studies that showcase how your product or service elevates users' status in their professional or personal life.

2. **Desire for Safety**: Create content that addresses concerns about health, financial security, or long-term stability. Provide assurances and evidence to back up claims.
3. **Desire for Belonging**: Foster a sense of community by engaging with your audience in ways that promote interaction and collaboration, such as social media challenges, user-generated content, or community forums.

Personalization and Relevance

Personalization is a powerful way to show your audience that you understand their desires. Using customer data, you can create personalised experiences tailored to individual preferences. For example, offering product recommendations based on past purchases or curating content around a user's browsing history can make them feel understood and valued.

At the same time, relevance is key. Stay attuned to your audience's shifting desires and current events that may influence them. If a global event affects your audience's safety or financial concerns, adjust your messaging to be empathetic and timely.

Key Takeaway:

Content that aligns with your audience's core desires builds trust, engagement, and loyalty. By understanding their emotional drivers, you can create more relevant, impactful, and personalized content.

4: Addressing Changing Desires

Desires are not static. What motivates your audience today might not be what motivates them next year. Market trends, technological advancements, and cultural shifts can all influence consumer desires. Therefore, it's crucial to continuously assess and adapt to these changes.

Keep Listening to Your Audience

Ongoing feedback loops, such as customer surveys, social media polls, and reviews, can help you track evolving desires. Always be open to feedback, whether it's positive or negative. This ongoing dialogue with your audience allows you to stay relevant and responsive to their changing needs.

Embrace Flexibility in Messaging

As desires change, so should your messaging. If your audience begins to prioritize sustainability, for example, adjusting your marketing to emphasize your brand's eco-friendly practices can keep you aligned with their values. Stubbornly sticking to outdated messaging will not only fail to engage your audience but can also alienate them.

Experiment and Innovate

Testing new ideas, formats, and approaches is a great way to stay ahead of shifting desires. A/B testing, for instance, can help you compare different messages to see which resonates more with your audience. Additionally, innovation in product features or customer experience can lead to a competitive advantage as desires evolve.

Key Takeaway:

Desires change over time, so it's essential to keep a finger on the pulse of your audience. Flexibility, continuous feedback, and experimentation are vital to staying relevant and meeting their evolving needs.

Conclusion: Aligning Your Strategy with Core Desires

Understanding your audience's core desires is not a one-time task; it's an ongoing process that requires careful listening, analysis, and adaptation. By diving into the psychology of desires, gathering relevant data, and continuously refining your approach, you can create content, products, and services that resonate on a deeper level.

The rewards for this effort are significant: increased engagement, brand loyalty, and customer satisfaction. When your audience feels that their core desires are understood and met, they are far more likely to connect with your brand, recommend it to others, and become repeat customers.

Ultimately, the businesses and creators who succeed in today's marketplace are those who go beyond surface-level needs and tap into the deeper desires that drive human behavior. By aligning your strategies with these core desires, you're not just selling products or providing content—you're fulfilling what matters most to your audience.

To create an irresistible offer, you must first understand who you're selling to. Every successful marketer understands the deep desires of their audience and leverages that knowledge to craft a message that speaks to the heart of what the buyer truly wants.

1. **Identify Emotional Triggers:** People buy emotionally and justify logically. Are they looking for status, security, or a transformation in their lives?
   Example: Apple doesn't just sell phones. They sell status, innovation, and a sleek lifestyle.
2. **Understand Their Problems:** The more urgent and pressing their problem, the more desperate they are for a solution. If you offer the right solution, you'll have them hooked.
   Example: Weight Watchers is successful not because they offer food advice, but because they offer a proven system to solve a deep emotional issue: weight loss and self-image.
3. **Focus on the Transformation, Not the Product:** People aren't buying the drill—they're buying the hole. Focus on what your product does for them, not what it is.

Quote: "The best marketers know that it's not about features or benefits, but about how you make the customer feel in the end." – Rohit Soni

Chapter 3

CREATING URGENCY AND SCARCITY IN MARKETING

In today's highly competitive market, creating urgency and scarcity has become one of the most effective tactics for marketers to drive quick decision-making, increase conversion rates, and enhance sales. When done correctly, these strategies tap into consumers' psychological triggers, encouraging them to act swiftly to avoid missing out on valuable opportunities. This chapter explores the principles of urgency and scarcity in marketing, why they work, how to implement them effectively, and some ethical considerations.

1: The Psychology Behind Urgency and Scarcity

Before we delve into the practical applications, it's crucial to understand the psychological mechanisms behind urgency and scarcity. These principles are deeply rooted in human psychology and behavior, making them incredibly potent in marketing.

Scarcity: The Fear of Missing Out (FOMO)

Scarcity operates on the basic economic principle of supply and demand: as availability decreases, perceived value increases. This is commonly referred to as the **scarcity principle** in psychology. When people perceive that a product or service is scarce, they are more likely to want it. Scarcity can manifest in different ways, including limited quantity, exclusive offers, and seasonal availability.

Psychologically, people fear loss more than they value gain. This is known as **loss aversion**—a concept in behavioral economics that highlights our preference for avoiding losses rather than acquiring equivalent gains. When customers feel that they might miss out on something valuable, they are more motivated to act quickly.

Urgency: The Pressure of Time

Urgency works by tapping into the human tendency to procrastinate unless there's a reason to act now. Urgency creates a time-sensitive situation where consumers feel they have a limited window to take advantage of an offer. This taps into the psychological principle of **temporal discounting**, where people value immediate rewards more highly than future rewards. As a result, time-limited offers compel consumers to act sooner rather than later.

Both urgency and scarcity activate emotional responses, making people feel compelled to make quicker decisions than they might otherwise. These emotional triggers, when ethically applied, can drive significant results in marketing campaigns.

Key Takeaway:

Scarcity and urgency are powerful because they tap into deep-seated psychological fears—fear of missing out and fear of loss. Understanding these principles helps marketers design campaigns that motivate consumers to take swift action.

2: Types of Scarcity and Urgency Tactics

There are different forms of scarcity and urgency, each serving a unique purpose depending on the context and target audience. Understanding these different types will help you apply the right strategy in your marketing campaigns.

Types of Scarcity

1. **Limited Quantity**: Limiting the number of items available increases their perceived value. For example, displaying "Only 5 left in stock!" or "Only 10 available for pre-order" encourages buyers to act fast before the product runs out.
2. **Exclusive Access**: Offering products or services to a specific group (e.g., VIP members, early adopters) creates a sense of exclusivity. Consumers feel privileged to access something others cannot, which motivates them to act before the offer is no longer available.
3. **Seasonal Scarcity**: This form of scarcity is created by limiting a product's availability to a particular season or time of year, such as holiday specials or limited-edition collections. Consumers know they

have a narrow window to purchase, increasing demand during that period.

4. **High Demand Messaging**: Indicating that a product is in high demand adds perceived value and urgency. For example, "Best-seller" or "Selling fast!" communicates that other consumers are buying, creating the social proof that encourages people to follow suit.

Types of Urgency

1. **Time-Limited Offers**: These are offers that expire after a specific period, such as "50% off for the next 24 hours" or "Ends at midnight!" The ticking clock creates a sense of urgency, pushing consumers to buy now rather than wait.
2. **Flash Sales**: Flash sales are short, intense promotions, usually lasting only a few hours. The immediacy of these events generates excitement and drives impulse purchases. Flash sales often feature significant discounts, increasing the incentive to act fast.
3. **Countdown Timers**: Countdown timers on websites or in marketing emails visually remind consumers how much time is left before an offer expires. The ticking clock adds a layer of pressure and immediacy, compelling shoppers to make quicker decisions.
4. **Event-Based Deadlines**: Tying offers to specific events (e.g., Black Friday, Cyber Monday, or a product launch) is a common tactic. Consumers

know these deals won't last, prompting them to make a purchase before the event ends.

Combining Scarcity and Urgency

For maximum impact, scarcity and urgency can be combined in your marketing efforts. For instance, promoting a limited-edition product that's only available for a short period ("Only 100 units available for 48 hours!") merges both tactics, creating a powerful psychological trigger that drives sales.

Key Takeaway:

By understanding the different types of scarcity and urgency, you can choose the most appropriate tactic for your product, audience, and marketing goals. Each approach, whether it's limiting quantity or offering time-sensitive discounts, capitalizes on the consumer's fear of missing out or losing an opportunity.

3: Implementing Urgency and Scarcity in Your Marketing Strategy

Now that we understand the psychological underpinnings and different types of urgency and scarcity, let's explore how to implement these strategies effectively in your marketing campaigns.

1. Create Real Scarcity

The most effective use of scarcity is grounded in reality. Consumers can spot false scarcity from a mile away, and using fake or manipulative scarcity can backfire, damaging your brand's credibility and consumer trust. For instance, if you claim that only 50 units are available when there are actually thousands, consumers may feel deceived once they find out.

Instead, base your scarcity on actual stock levels, limited-time product launches, or truly exclusive offers. If you're offering a limited edition, be transparent about its limitations. For digital products, scarcity could be tied to a limited number of licenses or access spots.

Example: Offering a limited number of tickets to an exclusive webinar or event ("Only 100 seats available—grab yours now!") creates genuine scarcity and motivates people to act quickly.

2. Use Personalization to Amplify Urgency

Tailoring urgency to individual consumers can significantly increase the effectiveness of your campaigns. E-commerce platforms and marketing automation tools allow you to track user behavior and create personalized experiences. For example, if a customer has left items in their shopping cart, an automated email reminder with a time-sensitive discount can nudge them toward completing the purchase.

Example: "Hurry! The items in your cart are selling fast. Complete your purchase in the next 2 hours to get 10% off!"

This personalized, behavior-based urgency taps into a customer's interest and uses the fear of missing out to drive conversion.

3. Leverage Social Proof Alongside Scarcity

Social proof—the idea that people look to others' behavior to guide their own—can be combined with scarcity to create a more compelling message. For example, showing that other people are purchasing the same item, especially in real-time, can enhance the perceived value and scarcity of the product.

Example: "3 people have purchased this item in the last 10 minutes!" or "Join 1,000 others who have already signed up."

This tactic not only highlights scarcity but also reinforces the desirability of the product by showing that others find it valuable.

4. Build a Sense of Exclusivity

Scarcity can be used to build a sense of exclusivity around your brand. Exclusive access to products or services creates a privileged feeling, making customers feel like they are part of an elite group. This technique works particularly well for membership sites, premium products, or early access to new releases.

Example: "Early access for our loyal customers—limited quantity available. Act fast before it goes public!"

By creating exclusivity, you position your product or service as something special that not everyone can have, which can drive quicker decision-making among your target audience.

5. Implement Urgency In Email Campaigns

Email marketing is a powerful tool for creating urgency and scarcity. You can use time-limited discounts, countdown timers, or exclusive offers to drive conversions directly from the inbox.

Example: "Don't miss out! 50% off ends in 24 hours. Click here to shop now."

Emails that highlight expiring deals or remind users of products they've shown interest in create a sense of urgency. Including visual elements like countdown timers in the email further amplifies the message.

6. Use Countdown Timers on Your Website

Countdown timers visually remind website visitors that time is running out, pushing them to take immediate action. Whether it's for a flash sale, limited-time discount, or product launch, timers create a tangible sense of urgency.

Example: A banner on your homepage that reads "Flash Sale! Ends in 02:59:15" with a live ticking countdown.

Countdown timers are particularly effective for e-commerce websites, where visitors are more likely to make impulse purchases when they see a deadline approaching.

7. Offer Limited-Time Bonuses

Another way to leverage urgency is by offering additional incentives for a limited time. This could include free shipping, an exclusive gift, or bonus content available only within a specific time frame. The temporary nature of the bonus encourages consumers to act immediately to take advantage of the extra value.

Example: "Order in the next 12 hours and receive a free gift with your purchase!"

Key Takeaway:

Effectively implementing scarcity and urgency in marketing requires thoughtful strategy and ethical consideration. Whether it's through personalized experiences, countdown timers

To create urgency and scarcity, you need to make the customer feel that the opportunity won't last forever.

1. **Limited-Time Offers:** The power of the ticking clock cannot be underestimated. When people think they'll miss out, they take action.
   Example: Every successful Kickstarter campaign includes a countdown. The message is clear: act now, or miss out.
2. **Limited Availability:** If there are only a few left, people will jump at the chance to own it.
   Example: Nike is a master at this. When they release a limited-edition sneaker, they sell out in minutes—because people know the supply is limited.
3. **Special Events or Occasions:** Tying your offer to a special event makes it feel like a unique opportunity.
   Example: Black Friday is the perfect example of this strategy in action. Stores create offers around the holiday that are "exclusive" and "unrepeatable."

Chapter 4

LEVERAGING SOCIAL PROOF IN MARKETING – THE DAN KENNEDY WAY

One of the most powerful tools in any marketer's arsenal is **social proof**. In today's world, where consumers are flooded with choices and often skeptical about marketing claims, social proof cuts through the noise. It offers a validation from others that what you're selling works. If you're a student of marketing, you know that **Dan Kennedy**, the master of direct response marketing, is a big advocate of strategies that not only sell but sell convincingly, using powerful psychological triggers like social proof. This chapter explores how to use social proof like Dan Kennedy—effectively, ethically, and with authority—to amplify your marketing, increase conversions, and build lasting trust with your audience.

1: Understanding Social Proof in Marketing

Social proof is the idea that people are more likely to take action when they see others doing the same. It's the phenomenon of **herd mentality**, where individuals tend to follow the actions and behaviours of a larger group. Dan Kennedy emphasises that people buy based on emotions, and then justify their decision with logic. Social proof plays into both emotions and logic. If people see that others have benefited from a product or service, they are emotionally reassured and can logically justify their purchase.

Why is social proof so important? In today's crowded and competitive marketplace, trust is at an all-time premium. People don't trust brands as easily as they used to, but they do trust **other people's experiences**—even if those people are complete strangers. Think about the last time you looked at a product on Amazon and scrolled down to read the reviews. You wanted reassurance that what you were about to buy was worth your money. Social proof provides this reassurance, making your marketing much more credible and compelling.

Dan Kennedy is a firm believer in **proof**. Proof is what makes or breaks a sale. Kennedy once said, "People aren't going to believe your claims unless you hammer them with irrefutable proof." In marketing, claims are easy, but evidence in the form of social proof is what will separate you from the hype-driven, snake oil salesmen. Social proof offers a form of real-world credibility that no fancy copywriting or flashy design can match.

Types of Social Proof:

1. **Customer Testimonials**: The bread and butter of social proof, testimonials come directly from satisfied customers. They show that your product or service has been tested and approved by real people. For Kennedy, testimonials are an essential tool because they give your potential customers a tangible sense of the benefits they can expect.

2. **Case Studies**: These go deeper than testimonials by showing detailed before-and-after scenarios, explaining exactly how your product or service solved a problem. Kennedy often stresses the power of case studies, particularly in high-ticket sales. They provide potential clients with a complete picture of how their investment will pay off.
3. **Social Media Proof**: Today, the power of platforms like Facebook, Instagram, and Twitter can't be ignored. User-generated content, comments, likes, and shares can provide potent social proof. Kennedy was quick to adopt new platforms as tools for creating direct response, and though he focused on more traditional methods, the value of online social proof isn't lost on modern marketers following his principles.
4. **Endorsements and Influencers**: Kennedy has always believed in leveraging authority figures—those who have influence over your audience. An endorsement from a celebrity, an expert, or an industry leader can be a massive credibility boost.
5. **Crowd Numbers**: Showcasing large numbers of satisfied customers, followers, or subscribers is another form of social proof. "Over 10,000 sold!" or "Join 50,000 happy subscribers!" helps assure potential customers that they're in good company.

Key Takeaway:

Dan Kennedy's focus on social proof is rooted in **building trust and credibility**. When you use social proof, you're giving your prospects permission to feel comfortable and confident in their decision to buy from you. You're aligning their emotions with the actions of others, which in turn leads to action on their part.

2: Building Credibility Through Customer Testimonials

If there's one thing Kennedy emphasizes time and time again, it's that **proof trumps promises**. You can promise the moon and stars, but without proof, your promises are just noise. Customer testimonials are among the most effective forms of proof you can use. In fact, they're so powerful that Kennedy often stresses that no piece of direct response marketing is complete without them.

How to Gather Effective Testimonials

Not all testimonials are created equal. Kennedy teaches that the more specific, emotional, and result-oriented a testimonial is, the more persuasive it will be. Vague testimonials like "Great product, I loved it!" aren't going to sway a skeptical audience. You need to drill deeper and get testimonials that address real problems and tangible results.

Example of a Weak Testimonial:

"Your service was great. I would recommend it to anyone."

Example of a Strong Testimonial (in the Kennedy style):

"I was skeptical at first, but after using this service for just two weeks, I increased my sales by 35%. Not only did the team overdeliver, but they provided ongoing support that helped me scale my business beyond what I thought was possible. If you're serious about growing your business, this is a no-brainer."

Kennedy suggests always asking your customers specific questions that will lead them to talk about measurable results. You want testimonials that speak to **the transformation** your product or service provided. A good testimonial makes prospects see themselves in the same position—before and after—and creates a compelling vision of the result they can achieve.

How to Use Testimonials Effectively

Kennedy knows how to make a testimonial pop. Don't just tuck them away on a "Testimonials" page where no one will see them. Instead, scatter them throughout your marketing—on your homepage, in sales emails, landing pages, and even in product descriptions.

Additionally, video testimonials can be particularly powerful, as they showcase genuine human emotion. Kennedy loves the concept of "authenticity," and there's no better way to convey authenticity than to hear and see someone genuinely speak about their positive experience.

Kennedy's Golden Rule for Testimonials

The more a testimonial resembles a **mini case study**, the more effective it is. Testimonials should focus on specific problems that were solved, measurable outcomes achieved, and the emotional benefit experienced by the customer. Kennedy's style is all about emphasizing **results**, and testimonials should clearly convey the results others have gotten with your product or service.

Key Takeaway:

In the Dan Kennedy way, testimonials are your most powerful **proof** that what you're offering works. They give your audience confidence, provide real-world validation, and make your marketing more believable and convincing.

3: Leveraging Case Studies for Maximum Impact

Dan Kennedy is a master of using case studies to **demonstrate value** and create compelling narratives that convince prospects to act. Unlike a short testimonial, a case study is a deep dive into how your product or service solved a significant problem for a customer. They provide undeniable proof that your solution delivers real, measurable results.

Crafting a Compelling Case Study

To create a persuasive case study, Kennedy recommends following a clear structure:

1. **Problem Identification**: Start by outlining the specific problem or challenge that your customer was facing before they used your product or service. This sets the stage and creates relatability for potential buyers who are likely facing similar issues.
2. **The Solution**: Explain how your product or service provided the solution. This is where you

demonstrate the key features and benefits, but be sure to avoid vague descriptions. Kennedy emphasizes specificity—be clear about what was done and why it worked.

3. **The Results**: This is the crux of the case study. Focus on quantifiable results: increases in revenue, cost savings, time saved, etc. For Kennedy, numbers are crucial. They provide undeniable proof that the product or service made a tangible difference.
4. **The Emotional Outcome**: Kennedy understands that all purchases are emotional at the core, even in B2B settings. Don't forget to include the emotional relief or happiness the customer felt once the problem was solved. Did they experience less stress? Were they finally able to meet a key deadline? Emotional outcomes are just as important as logical ones.

Example of a Strong Case Study:

"Before working with our agency, Client X was struggling with low traffic and poor conversion rates on their e-commerce site. They had tried various solutions, but nothing seemed to work. After implementing our strategic SEO plan, their site traffic increased by 45% in just three months. This led to a 30% increase in sales, and their conversion rate jumped from 2% to 5%. The client reported that not only did they see a dramatic uptick in sales, but they finally felt like they had control over their marketing strategy."

This case study shows a clear **before and after** scenario and uses **specific metrics** to prove the impact. Kennedy would argue that this is what turns potential buyers into actual customers—they can't argue with numbers and specific results.

Distributing Case Studies in Your Marketing

In Kennedy's style, you don't hide your best assets. Case studies shouldn't be buried on a page that no one sees. Instead, use them as direct marketing tools. Integrate them into your sales letters, email campaigns, and landing pages.

For instance, in an email sequence, you might send a case study to a warm lead who's close to making a decision but needs that final nudge. By showing them a detailed example of how someone just like them achieved significant results, you can push them to take action.

Additionally, Kennedy suggests using case studies in webinars or video sales letters. Walking through a real-world example step by step helps create a more engaging and persuasive narrative.

Key Takeaway:

Dan Kennedy teaches that case studies are one of the most powerful forms of social proof. They provide in-depth, irrefutable evidence that your product or service works, combining logic and emotion to persuade potential customers to buy.

4: Harnessing the Power of Social Media for Social Proof

Social media has taken the concept of social proof to a whole new level. While Dan Kennedy's classic marketing techniques were born in the era of direct mail and offline sales, the principles he espoused remain just as relevant in the digital world, particularly in the realm of social media.

The Role of User-Generated Content

One of the most authentic forms of social proof is **user-generated content** (UGC). This includes any content that customers create themselves, such as photos, videos, and reviews. Kennedy would tell you that when your audience becomes part of your marketing, they become a powerful asset in convincing others to join in. People trust recommendations from people they perceive as "just like them."

For example, if customers are sharing pictures of themselves using your product on Instagram, this is a form of organic social proof that can be far more persuasive than anything you might create yourself. Encourage this type of sharing by asking your customers to post about their experiences, and be sure to showcase this content on your own platforms.

Leveraging Online Reviews and Ratings

Platforms like Yelp, Google Reviews, and Amazon allow consumers to leave public reviews, which are highly influential forms of social proof. Kennedy would advise you to make it easy for satisfied customers to leave positive reviews by providing direct links and incentives like discounts or future offers.

More importantly, you should actively manage and respond to these reviews. Responding to both positive and negative reviews demonstrates that you care about your customers' experiences, which enhances your credibility.

Influencers as Modern-Day Endorsements

Kennedy has long been a fan of using **endorsements** from authoritative figures. In today's world, influencers—whether they're celebrities or micro-influencers with niche followings—play a similar role. Partnering with influencers who have authority in your market can create a powerful form of social proof that appeals to their followers.

However, it's important to ensure authenticity. Kennedy would stress the importance of integrity when it comes to endorsements. If an influencer genuinely believes in your product or service, their endorsement will come across as more genuine and trustworthy.

Key Takeaway:

Social media offers endless opportunities for leveraging social proof. Whether through user-generated content, online reviews, or influencer partnerships, these modern tools fit seamlessly into Kennedy's core marketing philosophy of using proof and authority to drive conversions.

5: Ethical Considerations and Long-Term Impact of Social Proof

Dan Kennedy is known for his no-nonsense approach to marketing, but he's also an advocate for ethical practices.

While social proof is highly effective, it's crucial to use it responsibly. Manipulating or fabricating social proof can lead to serious reputational damage and erode trust, which Kennedy would argue is one of your most valuable assets.

Authenticity Matters

Kennedy often speaks about the importance of **authenticity** in marketing. Using fake testimonials, inventing case studies, or artificially inflating numbers may provide short-term gains, but it can destroy your brand in the long run. Consumers today are savvier than ever, and they can quickly spot a marketing gimmick. Always ensure that the social proof you use is legitimate and aligns with your core values.

Building Long-Term Trust

When used correctly, social proof can build lasting trust with your audience. Kennedy stresses that trust is the foundation of any successful business relationship. The more real-world examples, testimonials, and case studies you can provide, the more your prospects will trust you. Trust leads to repeat customers, brand advocates, and, ultimately, a more profitable business.

Key Takeaway:

Dan Kennedy's approach to social proof is grounded in **ethical, results-driven marketing**. By using authentic social proof and focusing on long-term trust, you'll not only drive conversions but also create loyal customers who believe in your brand.

Conclusion: Making Social Proof a Core Part of Your Marketing

Social proof is an indispensable tool in your marketing toolkit, and Dan Kennedy's approach offers a blueprint for how to use it effectively. Whether you're leveraging testimonials, case studies, social media, or influencer endorsements, the key is to provide **proof** that your product or service delivers on its promises.

Remember, consumers are looking for reassurance that they're making the right decision. By providing them with ample evidence—whether it's in the form of glowing customer reviews or detailed case studies—you're not just selling a product; you're selling **confidence** in their purchase.

In true Kennedy fashion, always aim for **results-oriented marketing**. Every piece of social proof should point directly to the benefits and outcomes your customers can expect. And as you build a portfolio of satisfied customers, those customers will become your best marketing assets—driving more conversions and helping your business grow.

Final Key Takeaway:

Social proof is not a one-time tactic but a fundamental part of your long-term marketing strategy. By continually gathering and showcasing evidence that your product works, you'll build trust, authority, and, most importantly, a **profitable business**—the Dan Kennedy way.

People are more likely to buy if they see others doing the same. It's a fundamental part of human psychology—no one wants to miss out.

1. **Customer Testimonials:** Showing real-world success stories adds credibility to your offer.
   Example: Amazon dominates the online marketplace by displaying thousands of user reviews. Products with more positive reviews are perceived as more trustworthy.

2. **Influencer Endorsements:** If someone they admire or trust recommends your product, your prospect is more likely to act.
   Example: When Kylie Jenner promotes a new beauty product, her audience flocks to buy it—not necessarily because it's the best, but because she endorsed it.

3. **Case Studies:** Showcasing the results others have achieved using your product or service adds tremendous value.
   Example: B2B companies often use detailed case studies to show the ROI their clients achieved after working with them. These success stories are powerful motivators for prospective buyers.

Quote: "Social proof isn't just about credibility—it's about building trust through the collective experiences of others." – Rohit Soni

Chapter 5

THE PSYCHOLOGY OF PRICING AND VALUE IN DIGITAL MARKETING

In the fast-paced world of digital marketing, pricing plays a pivotal role in how consumers perceive the value of products and services. Price is more than just a number; it triggers psychological responses, shapes buying decisions, and influences consumer behavior. Marketers who understand the psychology behind pricing and value can craft pricing strategies that maximize profit, enhance perceived value, and build long-term customer relationships.

This chapter explores the psychological principles behind pricing, how to use these principles to influence consumer decisions, and practical pricing strategies to implement in your digital marketing efforts.

1: The Role of Price in Perceived Value

Price and value are intrinsically linked in the mind of the consumer. The price of a product or service is not just a reflection of its cost—it is a signal of its value. When people see a high price, they often associate it with higher quality, while lower prices can be interpreted as lower quality. This perception is deeply rooted in **anchoring** and **expectation theory**, two key concepts in behavioral economics.

The Power of Anchoring

Anchoring is a cognitive bias where people rely heavily on the first piece of information (the "anchor") when making decisions. In pricing, the anchor often becomes the first price a consumer encounters. Once a price is presented, all subsequent judgments are made relative to that price.

For example, when consumers see a luxury product priced at $1,000 and a mid-range product priced at $500, they perceive the $500 product as more affordable in comparison, even if they initially had no reference for what the product should cost. This is why higher-priced items can often make lower-priced alternatives appear more reasonable and affordable.

Marketers can use anchoring to their advantage by strategically setting reference prices that make their main offering look like a bargain. In digital marketing, this often manifests through tiered pricing models or "decoy" products, where one product is priced intentionally higher to make the next one down seem more valuable.

Expectation and Price as a Quality Signal

Consumers frequently use price as a proxy for quality, especially when other information about the product is limited. This concept is rooted in expectation theory, where consumers develop an expectation of quality based on price alone. For example, in an online store, if a handbag is priced at $50 and another at $500, many consumers will assume the more expensive one is better, even if they have no further information.

In digital marketing, this is crucial. When setting prices, you are not only indicating the cost of a product but also shaping the consumer's expectations of what they will receive in terms of quality, durability, and overall experience. Products priced too low may give the impression of being cheaply made, while premium pricing can create a perception of exclusivity and superior craftsmanship.

Key Takeaway:

Price is one of the most potent signals of value in digital marketing. Understanding anchoring and expectation theory allows you to set prices that not only maximize perceived value but also guide consumers toward the purchase decision you want them to make.

2: Pricing Strategies that Influence Consumer Behavior

The psychological impact of price goes beyond mere numbers. The way a price is structured, presented, and framed can significantly influence consumer decisions. Let's explore some of the most effective psychological pricing strategies that digital marketers can implement to improve conversions.

1. Charm Pricing (The Power of .99)

One of the simplest yet most effective pricing strategies is **charm pricing**, which involves ending prices in ".99" (e.g., $9.99 instead of $10.00). This pricing tactic is based on the principle of **left-digit bias**, where consumers focus more on the first digit in a price than the final digits.

For example, $9.99 feels closer to $9 than $10, even though the difference is only a penny. Studies show that consumers are more likely to buy products priced at $9.99 than those priced at $10.00 because they perceive the former as a better deal. This strategy leverages cognitive bias to make products seem more affordable and increase conversion rates.

2. The Decoy Effect

The **decoy effect** is another powerful psychological tool in pricing. This involves presenting a third, less attractive option to make one of the other two options seem more desirable. By offering a decoy product that is priced similarly to a higher-tier product but provides less value, marketers can push consumers toward the more valuable (and often more expensive) option.

For example, a subscription service might offer three tiers:

- Basic plan: $10 per month
- Premium plan: $30 per month
- Premium Plus plan: $32 per month

Here, the Premium Plus plan looks like a great deal compared to the Premium plan, since it offers significantly more value for only a small price increase. The decoy effect subtly nudges consumers to choose the more expensive option, leading to higher average revenue per customer.

3. Price Bundling

Price bundling is a strategy where several products or services are combined and sold as a single package at a lower price than the total cost of buying each item individually. This method leverages the psychological principle of **perceived value**—the consumer feels they are getting more for less.

In digital marketing, bundling is commonly used in software packages, online courses, and e-commerce. Offering a bundle allows you to boost sales by increasing the overall transaction size while giving the consumer a sense of getting a better deal.

For example, instead of selling three software tools individually for $50 each, a marketer might offer all three tools in a bundle for $120. The consumer perceives that they are saving $30, even though the company is increasing the overall sale value.

4. Price Framing and Discounts

Price framing refers to how you present a price in relation to a reference point. Framing can make prices seem more appealing by emphasizing what the consumer is saving or gaining.

For instance, showing a **discounted price** alongside the original price creates the illusion of getting a bargain, even if the original price was inflated. Phrases like "Originally $199, now only $99!" trigger a strong psychological response, making the consumer feel they are getting exceptional value.

Another powerful framing technique is highlighting the cost per day or per use. Instead of advertising a yearly subscription for $365, you might frame it as "Just $1 per day!" This breaks down the price into smaller, more digestible amounts, making the cost seem more manageable and less intimidating.

5. The "Free" Effect

Free is one of the most compelling words in marketing. When consumers see the word "free," it triggers a strong emotional response, and they are more likely to take action. The concept of getting something for free can override rational decision-making, leading to impulse purchases or sign-ups.

One effective way to use the free effect is through **free trials** or **free shipping** offers. By removing the upfront cost, consumers feel less risk in trying your product or service, which increases conversion rates. Once they've experienced the value of your product, they are more likely to commit to a paid plan or make repeat purchases.

Key Takeaway:

The way you structure and present prices can significantly impact how consumers perceive the value of your products and services. By using charm pricing, the decoy effect, price bundling, price framing, and the free effect, you can influence consumer behavior and drive conversions.

3: The Influence of Scarcity and Urgency on Pricing

Scarcity and urgency are powerful psychological drivers that can elevate the perceived value of a product and encourage quick purchasing decisions. By creating a sense of scarcity or urgency, marketers can push consumers to act before they miss out.

The Power of Scarcity in Pricing

Scarcity is a psychological principle based on the idea that people value things more when they are in limited supply. When a product is scarce, it triggers **FOMO (Fear of Missing Out)** and increases its perceived value.

There are several ways digital marketers can use scarcity in their pricing strategy:

- **Limited-time offers**: By offering a product or discount for a limited period, you encourage consumers to buy quickly before the offer expires.
- **Limited stock**: Displaying a message like "Only 5 items left in stock" creates a sense of urgency and increases the perceived value of the product, prompting consumers to act fast.
- **Exclusive pricing**: Offering exclusive deals to a select group of customers (e.g., email subscribers or VIP members) creates scarcity and a feeling of privilege, making customers feel they're getting something special.

Urgency as a Pricing Tactic

Urgency is closely related to scarcity, but instead of focusing on product availability, it revolves around time constraints. Creating a sense of urgency can prompt consumers to act quickly, as they fear losing out on a deal or opportunity.

In digital marketing, urgency can be effectively implemented through:

- **Flash sales**: Short-term sales with significant discounts create immediate urgency. Consumers know they must act fast to secure the deal.
- **Countdown timers**: Adding a countdown timer to your website or marketing emails can visually reinforce the limited time available for a special offer, further enhancing urgency.
- **Expiring discounts**: Highlighting that a discount or special pricing is about to expire creates the need to act now rather than later, increasing the likelihood of a purchase.

By combining scarcity and urgency in your pricing strategy, you create a psychological push that motivates consumers to act quickly, increasing conversion rates.

Key Takeaway:

Scarcity and urgency are potent psychological tools that can elevate the perceived value of your product and encourage immediate action. By creating limited-time offers, using countdown timers, and emphasising exclusivity, you can influence buying behaviour and drive sales.

4: The Role of Price Perception in Digital Products and Services

Pricing digital products and services presents unique challenges and opportunities. Unlike physical products, which have tangible attributes, digital goods are often intangible, which can make it harder for consumers to assess their value. As a result, **price perception** plays an even more critical role in digital marketing.

Value-Based Pricing for Digital Products

Value-based pricing is a strategy that sets the price of a product based on the perceived value to the customer rather than the cost of production. This is particularly effective for digital products like software, online courses, and subscriptions, where the cost to produce additional units is minimal.

To successfully implement value-based pricing, you must deeply understand your target audience's needs and pain points. The price should reflect the perceived benefit or outcome the consumer expects to receive from using your product. For example, a software tool that automates tasks and saves the user 10 hours per week could be priced higher than one that offers minimal time savings because the perceived value is greater.

Subscription Pricing Models

Subscription pricing has become one of the most popular pricing models in the digital world, especially for services like streaming platforms, SaaS products, and online communities. The psychology behind subscriptions revolves around **consistent value delivery** and reducing the perceived cost.

By breaking down the price into smaller, recurring payments (e.g., monthly or yearly fees), consumers perceive the service as more affordable and are less likely to experience "sticker shock." Moreover, subscriptions create a sense of ongoing value, as customers feel they are continuously benefiting from the service.

Freemium Models and Price Conversions

Many digital products, particularly software, utilise a **freemium model**, where the basic version of the product is offered for free, while premium features require a paid subscription. The psychology behind freemium models lies in the **endowment effect**—once consumers start using a product and derive value from it, they are more likely to upgrade to a paid plan.

Freemium models work by giving users a taste of the product's value, building trust and familiarity, and then introducing additional features or benefits that justify the price. The key is to strike a balance between offering enough free value to hook users while reserving enough premium features to incentivize them to pay.

Key Takeaway:

For digital products and services, pricing must be deeply aligned with perceived value. By using value-based pricing, subscription models, and freemium strategies, you can create a pricing structure that appeals to your target audience and drives long-term customer retention.

5: Ethical Considerations in Psychological Pricing

While psychological pricing strategies can be highly effective, they also come with ethical considerations. Manipulating pricing to take advantage of cognitive biases can lead to short-term gains but may erode trust over time if customers feel deceived. Ethical pricing ensures that while you leverage psychology to influence behavior, you do so transparently and in a way that builds long-term trust and loyalty.

Transparent Pricing Practices

One of the most important aspects of ethical pricing is **transparency**. Consumers today are savvier and more informed than ever, and they expect honesty in pricing. Misleading practices, such as hiding additional fees until checkout or inflating original prices to create false discounts, can damage your brand's reputation.

Instead, be upfront about your pricing. If you're offering a discount, make sure it's based on a genuine markdown from the original price. If there are additional costs, such as shipping or taxes, disclose them early in the purchasing process to avoid any surprises at checkout.

Avoiding Price Manipulation

Ethical pricing also means avoiding manipulation tactics that pressure consumers into making decisions they're not comfortable with. While urgency and scarcity can be powerful motivators, overusing these tactics or creating false scarcity (e.g., claiming there are only a few items left when there are plenty in stock) can backfire.

Instead, use scarcity and urgency authentically. If you're offering a limited-time deal, make sure it's genuinely limited. If a product is low in stock, communicate this truthfully. Building trust with your audience by being honest in your pricing will pay off in the long run, as customers are more likely to become loyal repeat buyers.

Key Takeaway:

Ethical pricing ensures that while you leverage psychological principles to influence consumer behavior, you do so transparently and in a way that builds long-term trust and loyalty.

Conclusion: The Strategic Role of Pricing in Digital Marketing

In digital marketing, pricing is much more than just a number. It's a powerful tool that shapes consumer perception, influences behavior, and drives conversions. By understanding the psychology behind pricing and value, marketers can create pricing strategies that align with consumer expectations, maximize perceived value, and increase sales.

Throughout this chapter, we've explored how psychological pricing techniques like anchoring, charm pricing, and the decoy effect can be used to guide consumers toward the desired purchase decision. We've also discussed how scarcity and urgency can create a sense of FOMO and drive immediate action.

However, it's essential to remember that pricing isn't just about short-term gains. Ethical pricing practices are crucial for building long-term trust with your audience. By being transparent and authentic in your pricing strategy, you can foster customer loyalty and create sustainable growth for your brand.

Ultimately, the key to effective pricing in digital marketing is understanding your audience's needs, desires, and pain points. When you align your pricing with the perceived value of your product or service, you're not just setting a price—you're creating a powerful psychological incentive that drives consumer behavior and boosts your bottom line.

Final Key Takeaway:

Pricing is one of the most powerful psychological tools in digital marketing. By mastering the principles of price perception, value, and consumer psychology, you can craft a pricing strategy that influences behavior, builds trust, and drives sustainable success for your brand.

Chapter 6

POSITIONING YOUR OFFER FOR MAXIMUM IMPACT

Positioning is a critical component of any successful marketing strategy. It's about shaping how your target audience perceives your product or service, and influencing where you stand in relation to your competitors. If your offer is positioned effectively, you don't just sell a product—you create an experience, a solution, or a transformation that resonates deeply with your audience.

This chapter will explore the intricacies of positioning, how to align your offer with customer needs, differentiate from competitors, and ensure that your offer creates maximum impact in the marketplace.

1: Understanding Positioning and Its Importance

Positioning is the process of defining your offer's unique place in the minds of your customers. It is about answering fundamental questions such as: Why should customers choose your product or service over others? What specific value do you bring that competitors don't? Effective positioning allows you to stand out in a crowded market, resonating with the people who need your solution most.

The Role of Positioning in Marketing

At its core, positioning is about perception. It's the story customers tell themselves about your offer, and the role it plays in their lives. This perception is shaped by multiple factors, including your messaging, brand, pricing, product features, and customer experience.

Positioning is crucial because it helps:

- **Define your niche**: Positioning helps you carve out a specific space in the market where your offer becomes the clear choice for a particular audience.
- **Differentiate from competitors**: It highlights what makes you different from your competitors, making it easier for customers to understand your value proposition.
- **Enhance brand loyalty**: When customers understand and resonate with your positioning, they're more likely to become loyal, repeat buyers.
- **Maximize relevance**: By aligning your positioning with your audience's desires and pain points, you can create a product or service that feels tailor-made for them.

How Positioning Impacts Consumer Perception

The way you position your offer affects how consumers perceive both your value and your brand. For instance, a high-end product positioned as a luxury item will create different expectations than one positioned as an affordable, everyday solution.

Consider the example of Apple vs. Samsung. Both companies offer smartphones, but Apple's positioning revolves around premium design, exclusivity, and an elevated user experience, while Samsung often positions itself as offering high-end technology at more competitive pricing. This subtle difference in positioning affects everything from their product development to marketing messages and customer loyalty.

The Positioning Statement

Your positioning statement is a concise way to communicate the core of your positioning strategy. It outlines who your target customer is, what need or problem you solve for them, and what makes your offer uniquely valuable compared to competitors.

A positioning statement often includes:

- **Target audience**: Who your offer is for.
- **Pain point or need**: The specific problem your offer solves or the desire it fulfills.
- **Unique selling proposition (USP)**: What makes your offer distinct from competitors.
- **Emotional or functional benefit**: How your offer benefits the customer on a practical or emotional level.

For example, if you're selling eco-friendly cleaning products, your positioning statement might be: "For environmentally-conscious households, our all-natural cleaning products offer a safe and effective solution without harmful chemicals—because a cleaner home shouldn't come at the cost of a cleaner planet."

Key Takeaway:

Positioning is the foundation of a successful marketing strategy. It defines your offer's unique value in the market, establishes differentiation, and ensures that your audience sees your product or service as the ideal solution to their problem.

2: Identifying and Understanding Your Target Audience

A critical component of positioning is knowing who your offer is for. If you don't have a deep understanding of your audience, it's nearly impossible to create a message that resonates or to position your product in a way that captures attention and drives action.

Creating Detailed Buyer Personas

Buyer personas are fictional representations of your ideal customers, based on real data about your existing customers and market research. These personas help you understand the demographic, psychographic, and behavioral characteristics of the people most likely to buy from you.

To create a useful buyer persona, ask yourself questions such as:

- What are their age, gender, and income level?
- What are their interests, values, and lifestyle preferences?
- What are their biggest challenges and pain points?
- What motivates them to make purchasing decisions?

- Where do they go for information or research before buying?

The more detailed your buyer personas, the better you can tailor your positioning to speak directly to their needs, desires, and problems. A well-defined persona ensures that every aspect of your marketing—from your messaging to product features—is designed with your ideal customer in mind.

Understanding Audience Pain Points

Once you've identified your target audience, it's crucial to dig into their **pain points**. Pain points are the problems, challenges, or unmet needs that your audience faces. The more clearly you understand these pain points, the better you can position your offer as the solution.

For instance, if you're marketing a fitness app, some pain points might include:

- Lack of time to go to the gym.
- Difficulty sticking to a workout routine.
- Limited knowledge of proper exercise techniques.

By identifying and understanding these pain points, you can position your fitness app as a convenient, easy-to-follow solution that fits seamlessly into a busy lifestyle. Your messaging might emphasize how your app offers personalized workout plans, instructional videos, and quick routines that can be done in 15 minutes.

Tailoring Your Message to Different Segments

Even within a target audience, there may be different segments with varying needs or priorities. Effective positioning often involves segmenting your audience and tailoring your message to each group.

For example, if you're selling eco-friendly products, one segment of your audience might be focused on sustainability and reducing waste, while another segment might be more concerned with the health benefits of using non-toxic materials. Your positioning should reflect these differences in priorities, allowing you to craft more compelling, relevant messages for each group.

Key Takeaway:

To position your offer for maximum impact, you need a deep understanding of your target audience. Creating detailed buyer personas and identifying your audience's pain points ensures that your positioning speaks directly to their needs, desires, and motivations.

3: Crafting a Unique Value Proposition

Your **Unique Value Proposition (UVP)** is the cornerstone of your positioning strategy. It's what sets you apart from the competition and tells your audience why they should choose your product or service over any other. A compelling UVP clearly communicates the unique benefit that your offer provides and how it addresses the specific needs of your target audience.

Defining Your Unique Value Proposition

A strong UVP answers these critical questions:

- **What problem do you solve?** Your UVP should clearly articulate the specific problem your product or service solves for your target audience.

- **What benefit do you offer?** Your UVP should highlight the main benefit that customers will experience when using your product.
- **How are you different from competitors?** Your UVP should differentiate you from competitors by focusing on what makes your offer unique or superior.

For example, Warby Parker's UVP is: "Try 5 frames for free at home. Pick your favorite, and we'll send you the prescription glasses. Free shipping both ways." This clearly addresses customer pain points (not being able to try on glasses before purchasing), offers a compelling benefit (free home try-ons), and sets them apart from traditional brick-and-mortar eyewear retailers.

The Role of Benefits in Your UVP

A common mistake in positioning is focusing too much on features rather than benefits. Features describe what your product does, while benefits explain why those features matter to the customer.

For example, let's say you're marketing a high-end blender. Features might include a powerful motor, multiple speed settings, and stainless steel blades. However, the benefits might be framed as:

- The powerful motor makes blending quicker, saving you time.
- Multiple speed settings allow for customized texture, ensuring perfect smoothies every time.
- Stainless steel blades provide durability, so you can use the blender for years without replacement.

Your UVP should always focus on the benefits, answering the customer's unspoken question: "What's in it for me?"

Differentiating from Competitors

Your UVP should not only highlight the benefits of your product or service but also differentiate you from competitors. In a saturated market, standing out is crucial. You need to communicate why your offer is better, more valuable, or different in a meaningful way.

Some ways to differentiate include:

- **Product innovation**: Offering a feature or technology that no one else does.
- **Pricing**: Providing better value for money or creating premium pricing for an exclusive experience.
- **Customer experience**: Delivering a superior buying or usage experience, such as exceptional customer service or faster delivery.
- **Niche focus**: Specializing in a specific market or addressing a unique pain point that competitors overlook.

For example, Tesla's UVP revolves around the combination of high-performance electric vehicles with cutting-edge technology and a commitment to sustainability. This positions them uniquely in the automotive market, differentiating them from both traditional car manufacturers and other electric vehicle makers.

Key Takeaway:

Your UVP is the heart of your positioning strategy. It clearly articulates what makes your product or service unique, how it solves a problem, and why customers should choose you over the competition.

4: Differentiating Your Offer from the Competition

In a crowded marketplace, differentiation is essential. Consumers are bombarded with choices, and if your offer doesn't stand out, it will get lost in the noise. Your differentiation strategy should focus on what makes your product or service unique, valuable, and better than the competition.

Identifying Competitor Strengths and Weaknesses

To effectively differentiate your offer, you first need to understand where your competitors stand. Conducting a **competitive analysis** allows you to identify their strengths, weaknesses, and market positioning. This information helps you identify gaps or opportunities where your offer can stand out.

Some ways to analyze competitors include:

- **Pricing models**: What pricing strategies do your competitors use? Are they positioned as affordable, premium, or somewhere in between?
- **Product features**: What features do their products or services offer? How do they compare to yours?
- **Customer reviews**: What do customers like or dislike about your competitors? Reading reviews on third-party websites or social media can reveal pain points that you can address in your own positioning.

- **Marketing messaging**: How do competitors present themselves in their ads, website copy, and social media? What tone do they use, and what audience are they targeting?

For example, if you discover that a competitor's customers are frequently frustrated by poor customer service, you can position your business as the company that delivers exceptional, responsive support, using that differentiation as a key selling point.

Creating a Niche Market

One of the most effective ways to differentiate is by carving out a niche market. Instead of trying to appeal to a broad audience, focus on a specific group of customers with unique needs or preferences. Niching down allows you to tailor your product and messaging to a well-defined audience, creating a stronger connection and offering a more relevant solution.

For example, if you sell athletic apparel, instead of targeting all athletes, you could focus specifically on yoga enthusiasts who value eco-friendly, sustainable fabrics. By focusing on a niche, you become the go-to brand for that specific audience.

Building a Brand Story Around Your Differentiation

Your brand story plays a crucial role in how you differentiate your offer. A compelling brand story helps customers understand what you stand for, why you exist, and how you're different from others in the market. It provides context for your product and gives customers a reason to care.

For example, TOMS Shoes differentiates itself through its "One for One" business model, where for every pair of shoes sold, a pair is donated to someone in need. This brand story resonates with socially-conscious consumers and sets TOMS apart from other footwear brands.

To build your brand story, consider:

- **Your mission**: What is the larger purpose behind your business?
- **Your origin**: How did your product or service come to be? Was it created to solve a personal problem or fill a gap in the market?
- **Your values**: What does your brand stand for, and how do these values resonate with your target audience?

A strong brand story not only differentiates you from competitors but also builds emotional connections with customers, driving loyalty and advocacy.

Key Takeaway:

Differentiating your offer is critical to standing out in a crowded market. By conducting a competitive analysis, targeting a niche market, and building a compelling brand story, you can create a unique and valuable position that resonates with your audience.

5: Testing and Refining Your Positioning for Maximum Impact

Positioning is not a one-time effort. The market, consumer preferences, and competitors are constantly evolving, which means your positioning needs to be adaptable. Continuous testing, refinement, and optimization are essential to ensure that your positioning remains relevant, impactful, and effective.

Testing Your Positioning

Once you've developed your positioning, it's important to test it in the real world. Testing allows you to gather feedback, measure how well your message resonates with your audience, and identify areas for improvement.

Some ways to test your positioning include:

- **Surveys and feedback**: Ask your customers or target audience for feedback on your positioning. Do they understand your value proposition? Does your messaging resonate with them? What aspects of your offer do they find most compelling?
- **A/B testing**: Run A/B tests on different elements of your positioning, such as your tagline, product description, or value proposition. By comparing different variations, you can see which version performs better and resonates more with your audience.
- **Customer interviews**: Conduct in-depth interviews with your customers to gain insights into how they perceive your brand and why they chose your product or service over competitors.

For example, if you're positioning a meal delivery service as "healthy and convenient," you might A/B test different taglines such as "Fuel Your Day with Nutritious

Meals" vs. "Healthy Eating, Delivered to Your Door." By measuring the response to each message, you can refine your positioning for maximum impact.

Refining Your Positioning Over Time

As your business grows and the market changes, you may need to adjust your positioning. This could be due to shifts in consumer behavior, the emergence of new competitors, or the evolution of your product offerings. Regularly reviewing and refining your positioning ensures that it stays relevant and resonates with your target audience.

For example, if a new competitor enters the market offering similar products at a lower price point, you may need to shift your positioning to focus more on the quality, premium materials, or customer experience that differentiates your offer.

Additionally, as your product or service evolves, your positioning may need to reflect new features or benefits. For instance, if you introduce new features to your software platform that address additional pain points, your positioning should highlight these new benefits to keep your audience engaged and aware of your evolving value proposition.

The Role of Data in Positioning

Data plays a critical role in refining your positioning. By analyzing customer behavior, sales trends, and market data, you can identify what's working and what's not in your current strategy.

Metrics to track include:

- **Conversion rates**: Are people responding to your marketing messages and converting into customers?
- **Customer retention**: Are customers sticking around, or are they leaving after their first purchase?
- **Brand sentiment**: What are people saying about your brand online? Are they talking about the specific aspects of your offer that you've positioned as unique or valuable?

By analyzing these metrics, you can make data-driven decisions about how to adjust your positioning for maximum impact.

Key Takeaway:

Positioning is not static—it requires ongoing testing, refinement, and optimization. By gathering feedback, testing different messages, and analyzing data, you can ensure that your positioning continues to resonate with your audience and drive results.

Conclusion: Positioning for Long-Term Success

Positioning your offer for maximum impact is one of the most critical aspects of building a successful brand and driving long-term growth. A well-positioned offer not only stands out in a crowded market but also creates lasting connections with your target audience.

Throughout this chapter, we've explored the importance of positioning, how to identify and understand your audience, and how to craft a compelling unique value proposition. We've also discussed the importance of differentiation and how to continuously refine your positioning to ensure that it remains effective and impactful.

Ultimately, the key to successful positioning is understanding your audience's needs, delivering a clear and compelling value proposition, and differentiating your offer in a way that resonates with your customers. Positioning is not just about what you sell—it's about how you communicate your value, solve problems, and build a brand that people trust and love.

As you refine your positioning strategy over time, remember that the most successful brands are those that stay true to their core values, listen to their customers, and adapt to the changing landscape. By positioning your offer effectively, you'll create a strong foundation for growth, build lasting customer relationships, and maximize your impact in the marketplace.

Final Key Takeaway:

Positioning is a dynamic, ongoing process that requires deep understanding of your audience, clear differentiation from competitors, and continuous refinement. When done right, it creates lasting value, builds brand loyalty, and drives long-term success.

Chapter 7

BONUSES, GUARANTEES, AND RISK REVERSAL IN INTERNET MARKETING

In the world of internet marketing, consumers are constantly bombarded with offers, discounts, and promotions. With so many options available, it can be challenging for any product or service to stand out. However, marketers who understand the psychological triggers that drive buying decisions know that a well-crafted offer can make all the difference. Two of the most powerful tools you can use to elevate your offer are **bonuses** and **guarantees**. Additionally, implementing effective **risk reversal** strategies can eliminate potential barriers to purchase, turning hesitant prospects into paying customers.

This chapter explores how to use bonuses, guarantees, and risk reversal effectively in internet marketing, providing actionable insights and real-world examples of how these tactics can boost conversions, build trust, and drive long-term success.

1: The Power of Bonuses in Internet Marketing

When it comes to creating irresistible offers, bonuses play a pivotal role. A **bonus** is an additional item, service, or benefit that is offered as part of a purchase, providing extra value beyond the core offer. Bonuses create a sense of urgency and exclusivity, which can motivate potential customers to take immediate action.

Why Bonuses Work

Bonuses work because they tap into the psychological principle of **reciprocity**. According to this principle, when someone gives you something of value, you feel a natural inclination to give something in return. In marketing, this often translates to a purchase. Offering a valuable bonus makes the customer feel like they are getting more than they bargained for, which increases the perceived value of the core product or service.

Additionally, bonuses can:

- **Differentiate your offer** from competitors who may sell similar products or services.
- **Increase perceived value**, making the main offer appear more attractive without discounting the price.
- **Create urgency** by offering time-sensitive bonuses that expire if the customer doesn't act quickly.

Types of Effective Bonuses

1. **Complementary Products or Services**: A bonus that complements the main offer enhances the customer's overall experience. For example, if you're selling an online course on social media marketing, you might offer a bonus eBook on content creation or access to a private community for ongoing support.

2. **Exclusive Access**: Offering something exclusive, such as a limited-time webinar, live Q&A session, or one-on-one consultation, creates scarcity and makes the bonus feel special. This sense of exclusivity can drive prospects to buy sooner rather than later.
3. **Digital Downloads**: In the world of internet marketing, digital bonuses are especially effective because they can be delivered instantly, with little to no additional cost to the marketer. EBooks, checklists, templates, and software tools are all examples of bonuses that provide added value.
4. **Physical Goods**: While digital products are common, physical bonuses can also create a tangible sense of value. For example, if you're selling a high-ticket program, you might offer a physical welcome kit or book that enhances the customer's experience.

Structuring Bonuses for Maximum Impact

The key to using bonuses effectively is to ensure that they add value without overwhelming the customer. Offering too many bonuses can dilute the impact of the main offer or make the purchase decision confusing. Here are some guidelines for structuring bonuses:

- **Relevance**: Make sure the bonus is highly relevant to the main offer. If the bonus feels disconnected or irrelevant, it will not enhance the customer's perception of value.
- **Scarcity and Urgency**: Use time-sensitive language such as "This bonus is available for the first

100 customers" or "Only available until midnight." Scarcity creates urgency and motivates buyers to take action quickly.

- **Clarity**: Clearly communicate the value of the bonus. Assign a dollar value to the bonus (e.g., "This $299 value is yours free when you purchase today") to help customers understand its worth.

Examples of Successful Bonus Strategies

1. **Russell Brunson and ClickFunnels**: Internet marketing expert Russell Brunson uses bonuses effectively in his sales funnels. For example, when purchasing ClickFunnels, users often get a bonus package that includes training courses, templates, and live coaching. This increases the perceived value of the software, making it a no-brainer for customers.
2. **Amy Porterfield's Online Course Launches**: Amy Porterfield, a well-known online course creator, often adds bonuses to her course launches, such as exclusive templates, additional modules, or VIP access to live events. These bonuses are designed to remove barriers to success, giving customers everything they need to implement what they've learned.

Key Takeaway:

Bonuses enhance the perceived value of your offer, create urgency, and differentiate you from competitors. When used strategically, they can significantly increase conversion rates by giving customers additional reasons to act now.

2: The Role of Guarantees in Building Trust and Reducing Risk

A **guarantee** is one of the most powerful tools a marketer can use to build trust and overcome objections. In internet marketing, where customers can't physically interact with a product before buying, guarantees serve as a safety net, giving buyers peace of mind that their purchase is protected.

Why Guarantees Work

Guarantees tap into the psychological principle of **risk aversion**. Consumers are naturally wary of making a bad purchase decision, especially in the online space where trust can be harder to establish. A strong guarantee eliminates or reduces the perceived risk, making it easier for customers to move forward with a purchase.

There are several reasons guarantees are effective:

- **They build trust**: Offering a guarantee signals that you stand behind your product and are confident in its value.
- **They reduce buyer anxiety**: Customers feel more comfortable making a purchase if they know they can get their money back if they aren't satisfied.
- **They increase conversion rates**: When customers know they have nothing to lose, they are more likely to take action.

Types of Guarantees

1. **Money-Back Guarantee**: This is the most common type of guarantee, offering customers a refund if

they are not satisfied with their purchase. Common time frames include 30 days, 60 days, or 90 days, depending on the product or service.

   - **Example**: "Try our software for 30 days, and if you don't see results, we'll give you a full refund—no questions asked."

2. **Satisfaction Guarantee**: This type of guarantee promises that the product or service will meet the customer's expectations. If not, the customer can receive a refund or other compensation.
   - **Example**: "We guarantee that our meal plan will help you lose weight within 30 days, or your money back."
3. **Lifetime Guarantee**: For physical products, offering a lifetime guarantee can be a powerful way to build long-term trust with customers. This guarantee promises that the product will last, and if it doesn't, the company will replace or repair it.
   - **Example**: "We stand behind our watches for life. If it ever breaks, we'll repair or replace it—no questions asked."
4. **Conditional Guarantee**: A conditional guarantee adds an extra layer of protection but requires the customer to meet certain criteria. For example, a weight-loss program might offer a refund only if the customer follows the program and doesn't achieve results.
   - **Example**: "Follow our step-by-step system for 90 days, and if you don't lose at least 10 pounds, we'll give you a full refund."

How to Craft an Effective Guarantee

A well-crafted guarantee can boost your credibility and increase sales, but it must be structured carefully to avoid potential downsides, such as abuse or excessive returns. Here are some tips for crafting an effective guarantee:

- **Be specific**: A vague guarantee lacks credibility. Be clear about what you're promising and under what conditions the guarantee applies.
- **Remove risk**: Your guarantee should eliminate as much risk as possible for the customer. The lower the perceived risk, the higher the likelihood of purchase.
- **Length of guarantee**: While a 30-day money-back guarantee is standard, longer guarantees (e.g., 60 days or 90 days) can reduce pressure on the customer and give them more confidence in their decision.

Real-World Examples of Successful Guarantees

1. **Zappos**: The online shoe retailer Zappos became famous for its **365-day return policy**. Customers have a full year to return their shoes, which eliminates any hesitation around purchasing footwear online. Zappos' generous guarantee helped establish the company as a trusted leader in e-commerce.
2. **Warby Parker**: Warby Parker offers a **30-day satisfaction guarantee** on their glasses. Additionally, they offer a **free home try-on program**, allowing customers to try on up to five pairs of glasses at home before committing to a purchase.

This dual guarantee reduces risk and makes online shopping for glasses more convenient.

Key Takeaway:

Guarantees eliminate risk and build trust with your audience. When customers know that their purchase is protected, they're more likely to take action, leading to higher conversions and sales.

3: Mastering Risk Reversal in Internet Marketing

Risk reversal is a powerful psychological strategy that removes or shifts the perceived risk of a transaction from the customer to the seller. By taking on the risk, you make it easier for customers to say "yes" to your offer, knowing that they won't suffer negative consequences if they're not satisfied.

What is Risk Reversal?

In a traditional sales transaction, the customer bears the majority of the risk. They pay money upfront, and if the product doesn't meet their expectations, they may feel stuck with a bad deal. Risk reversal turns this dynamic on its head by shifting the risk to the seller, creating a sense of security for the buyer.

Risk reversal strategies go beyond simple guarantees and can take many forms, depending on the product or service being offered.

The Psychology Behind Risk Reversal

Risk reversal works because it leverages **loss aversion**, a well-documented psychological phenomenon that shows people fear losses more than they value equivalent gains. For example, the pain of losing $100 feels stronger than the joy of gaining $100. Risk reversal neutralizes this fear by assuring the customer that they have nothing to lose.

In internet marketing, risk reversal is particularly important because customers can't physically interact with products before buying. The lack of tangibility creates more uncertainty, making it crucial for marketers to offer reassurances that minimize perceived risk.

Types of Risk Reversal Strategies

1. **Free Trials**: One of the most effective forms of risk reversal is offering a free trial. A free trial lets customers experience your product or service firsthand, without any financial commitment, before deciding whether to continue. This works especially well for SaaS products, subscription services, and digital products.
    - **Example**: Netflix offers a **30-day free trial**, allowing users to explore their streaming service before paying. This risk-free entry point has been instrumental in driving subscriber growth.
2. **Pay Later Models**: Offering a "pay later" model allows customers to use your product or service for a period of time before they are billed. This removes

the immediate financial risk and gives them time to see if the product meets their expectations.

   - **Example**: Afterpay, a service that allows customers to "buy now, pay later," has gained immense popularity by enabling shoppers to receive their products before paying in full. This model reduces the upfront financial burden and increases conversions.

3. **Performance Guarantees**: A performance guarantee promises specific results or outcomes, reducing the customer's perceived risk of wasting money. If the product or service doesn't deliver on the promised result, the customer can get a refund or additional compensation.
   - **Example**: A marketing agency might offer a performance-based guarantee, such as "Increase your website traffic by 20% within 90 days, or you don't pay."
4. **Warranties and Service Guarantees**: For physical products, offering warranties or service guarantees can provide customers with confidence that their purchase is protected over the long term. This form of risk reversal is particularly useful for high-ticket items or products with complex functionality.
   - **Example**: Apple offers a one-year warranty on all its devices, as well as the option to purchase **AppleCare+**, which provides extended coverage. This risk reversal strategy gives customers peace of mind, knowing that any issues with their expensive purchase will be taken care of.

Structuring Risk Reversal for Maximum Effectiveness

For risk reversal to be effective, it needs to be structured in a way that genuinely reduces or eliminates customer concerns. Here are some tips for implementing risk reversal:

- **Make it simple**: The easier it is for customers to understand and take advantage of your risk reversal offer, the more effective it will be. Avoid complicated terms and conditions that create friction in the process.
- **Be bold**: The more generous and confident your risk reversal strategy is, the more powerful it will be. For example, offering a **lifetime guarantee** on a product sends a strong message that you believe in its quality.
- **Combine with other tactics**: Risk reversal works even better when paired with other psychological triggers, such as bonuses or guarantees. For example, offering a **free trial** with a money-back guarantee can remove nearly all risk for the customer.

Real-World Examples of Risk Reversal in Action

1. **Basecamp**: The project management software Basecamp offers a **30-day free trial** with no credit card required. This makes it easy for potential customers to sign up and use the software without any financial commitment, reducing the perceived risk of trying a new platform.
2. **Domino's Pizza**: In the 1980s, Domino's Pizza famously ran a campaign offering **30 minutes or**

it's free. This performance guarantee not only differentiated Domino's from competitors but also removed the risk of late delivery for customers, positioning the brand as reliable and fast.

Key Takeaway:

Risk reversal shifts the burden of risk from the customer to the seller, making it easier for prospects to say "yes" to your offer. Whether through free trials, performance guarantees, or pay-later models, risk reversal can dramatically increase conversions and build trust with your audience.

4: Combining Bonuses, Guarantees, and Risk Reversal for Maximum Impact

While bonuses, guarantees, and risk reversal are powerful tools on their own, they become even more effective when used together. By combining these strategies, you can create a compelling, irresistible offer that addresses customer objections, maximizes perceived value, and reduces the risk of making a purchase.

How These Strategies Work Together

1. **Bonuses Enhance the Core Offer**: Bonuses increase the perceived value of your offer by providing additional resources, products, or services that complement the main purchase. By adding bonuses, you create a sense of urgency and exclusivity that motivates customers to act quickly.
2. **Guarantees Eliminate Risk**: Guarantees provide a safety net for customers, assuring them that if they

are not satisfied, they won't lose their money. This helps reduce anxiety around making a purchase, especially for higher-priced items or services.

3. **Risk Reversal Removes Barriers**: Risk reversal strategies, such as free trials or performance guarantees, eliminate the risk of trying your product. When combined with a strong guarantee and added bonuses, risk reversal makes it almost impossible for customers to say "no."

Structuring the Ultimate Offer

To create a high-converting offer using bonuses, guarantees, and risk reversal, follow these steps:

1. **Create a Valuable Core Offer**: Start with a product or service that delivers real value. Your offer should solve a specific problem or meet a pressing need for your audience.
2. **Add Relevant, High-Value Bonuses**: Choose bonuses that enhance the customer's experience with the core offer. These bonuses should be relevant, practical, and easy to implement. Assign a dollar value to the bonuses to highlight the extra value customers are receiving.
3. **Offer a Strong Guarantee**: Include a generous guarantee that removes risk for the customer. A 30-day or 60-day money-back guarantee is standard, but don't be afraid to go further if you're confident in your product.
4. **Incorporate Risk Reversal**: Use a free trial, pay-later model, or performance guarantee to eliminate

risk. This reassures customers that they have nothing to lose by trying your product or service.

5. **Create Scarcity or Urgency**: Introduce a sense of urgency by limiting the availability of bonuses or using time-sensitive language. For example, offer the bonus package only to the first 100 customers or for a limited time, such as 48 hours.

Real-World Example: The All-Inclusive Offer

Let's say you're selling an online fitness program. Here's how you could structure an offer using bonuses, guarantees, and risk reversal:

- **Core Offer**: A 12-week fitness training program with video tutorials, workout plans, and nutrition guides.
- **Bonus 1**: A meal prep guide with recipes and shopping lists ($50 value).
- **Bonus 2**: Access to a private Facebook group for accountability and support ($100 value).
- **Bonus 3**: A one-on-one virtual consultation with a fitness coach ($200 value).
- **Guarantee**: A 60-day money-back guarantee if the customer doesn't see results.
- **Risk Reversal**: A 7-day free trial with full access to the program before any payment is required.
- **Scarcity**: Bonuses are only available to the first 100 customers or until midnight on a specific date.

This comprehensive offer not only adds immense value through bonuses but also reduces risk through a strong guarantee and free trial, while creating urgency with limited-time availability.

Key Takeaway:

Combining bonuses, guarantees, and risk reversal into a single offer creates an irresistible proposition for potential customers. By increasing perceived value, eliminating risk, and adding urgency, you can significantly boost conversions and create a winning offer that stands out in the marketplace.

Conclusion: Leveraging Bonuses, Guarantees, and Risk Reversal for Long-Term Success

Bonuses, guarantees, and risk reversal are essential components of any successful internet marketing strategy. Together, they help build trust, reduce perceived risk, and increase the perceived value of your offer. When used correctly, these strategies not only boost conversions but also improve customer satisfaction and loyalty.

Throughout this chapter, we've explored the psychology behind these tactics, how to structure them effectively, and real-world examples of how they can be implemented in various marketing scenarios.

Recap of Key Strategies:

- **Bonuses**: Enhance the perceived value of your offer by adding relevant, high-value bonuses that complement the core product or service. Use scarcity and urgency to encourage immediate action.
- **Guarantees**: Eliminate risk by offering strong guarantees, such as money-back promises,

satisfaction guarantees, or performance guarantees. Make your customers feel secure in their decision to buy.

- **Risk Reversal**: Shift the perceived risk from the customer to the seller through free trials, pay-later models, or warranties. This removes barriers to purchase and encourages customers to try your product or service without fear of loss.

As you continue to refine your internet marketing efforts, remember that these strategies are not one-size-fits-all. Tailor them to your specific audience, product, and market conditions to maximize their effectiveness. The goal is to create offers that your customers can't refuse, making it easy for them to say YES.

Chapter 8

WRITING COMPELLING COPY THAT CONVERTS

Crafting compelling copy is essential to grabbing attention, engaging your audience, and driving conversions. Compelling copy is more than just creative wordplay—it's about strategically communicating your message in a way that resonates with your audience, solves their problems, and prompts them to take action. Whether you're writing for a sales page, email marketing, or social media ads, the right copy can make all the difference.

In this chapter, we'll break down the key principles of writing copy that converts, exploring the psychological triggers that influence buying behavior, proven frameworks, and actionable tips for creating copy that turns readers into buyers.

1: Understanding Your Audience

The foundation of compelling copy is a deep understanding of your target audience. To write copy that converts, you must first know who you're speaking to. The more intimately you understand your audience's needs, desires, and pain points, the better you can craft messages that resonate with them.

Creating Buyer Personas

A **buyer persona** is a fictional representation of your ideal customer, based on real data and research. Developing detailed buyer personas helps you understand who your audience is and how to speak to them effectively.

When building your buyer personas, consider the following:

- **Demographics**: Age, gender, location, education, and income.
- **Psychographics**: Interests, values, lifestyle, and personality traits.
- **Pain points**: What challenges or problems does your audience face? What frustrations or unmet needs do they have?
- **Motivations**: What are their goals? What benefits are they seeking, and what motivates them to make a purchase?
- **Buying behavior**: How do they typically research and make purchasing decisions? What objections might they have?

By developing these personas, you can craft copy that speaks directly to your target audience, addressing their pain points and desires while positioning your product or service as the solution they need.

Speaking to Pain Points

People buy solutions to their problems. To write compelling copy, you must identify your audience's most pressing pain points and show how your product or service solves them. Focus on the **benefits** of your offer, not just the features. For example, if you're selling a project management tool, instead of just listing features like "task organization" or "team collaboration," highlight the benefits: "Save hours of time each week by keeping your team on the same page and never missing a deadline again."

Key Takeaway:

The more you know your audience, the more effectively you can speak to their needs. Tailoring your copy to address specific pain points and desires creates a strong emotional connection, increasing the likelihood of conversion.

2: The Psychology of Persuasion in Copywriting

Compelling copy doesn't just inform—it persuades. To write copy that converts, you need to understand the psychological triggers that influence buying decisions. Here are some of the most powerful psychological principles you can use to craft persuasive copy.

1. Reciprocity

People are naturally inclined to return favors. When you give something valuable to your audience—such as a free guide, discount, or valuable information—they're more likely to reciprocate by purchasing your product or engaging with your offer.

How to use it: Offer free resources or valuable information in your marketing, such as a free eBook, checklist, or webinar. By giving value upfront, you build trust and increase the likelihood of conversion later.

2. Social Proof

Social proof is the concept that people look to others when making decisions. Seeing others' positive experiences with your product or service reassures potential customers that they're making the right choice.

How to use it: Incorporate testimonials, case studies, reviews, and user-generated content in your copy. Highlighting the experiences of satisfied customers builds trust and encourages new prospects to follow suit.

3. Scarcity

Scarcity creates urgency. When people believe that something is in limited supply or only available for a short time, they're more likely to act quickly to avoid missing out.

How to use it: Use phrases like "limited-time offer," "only a few spots left," or "while supplies last" in your copy to create urgency and prompt immediate action.

4. Authority

Consumers are more likely to trust and purchase from brands they perceive as authoritative or knowledgeable. When you position yourself as an expert in your field, your audience feels more confident in their decision to buy from you.

How to use it: Establish your authority by sharing credentials, awards, media mentions, or highlighting your experience. Using authoritative language in your copy, such as "trusted by over 10,000 customers" or "featured in Forbes," boosts credibility.

5. FOMO (Fear of Missing Out)

People hate missing out on valuable opportunities. The fear of missing out is a strong motivator that can push prospects to take action quickly before they lose out on something.

How to use it: Incorporate FOMO into your copy by showcasing limited-time discounts, exclusive offers, or bonuses that will disappear if they don't act now.

Key Takeaway:

Leveraging psychological triggers like reciprocity, social proof, scarcity, authority, and FOMO makes your copy more persuasive. Understanding these principles and applying them strategically can significantly boost conversions.

3: Using Proven Copywriting Frameworks

Copywriting frameworks are time-tested structures that guide your audience through the buying process. These frameworks help you organize your message in a way that captures attention, builds interest, and encourages action.

1. The AIDA Formula (Attention, Interest, Desire, Action)

The AIDA formula is one of the most widely used frameworks in copywriting, designed to lead readers from initial interest to final action.

- **Attention**: Grab the reader's attention with a compelling headline or opening statement.
- **Interest**: Build interest by expanding on the problem or need that your product or service addresses.
- **Desire**: Create desire by highlighting the benefits and outcomes of your offer.
- **Action**: Close with a clear, compelling call to action that tells the reader exactly what to do next.

2. PAS (Problem, Agitate, Solve)

The PAS formula focuses on identifying the reader's problem, amplifying the emotional discomfort it causes, and then positioning your product or service as the solution.

- **Problem**: Clearly define the problem your audience is facing.
- **Agitate**: Agitate the problem by emphasizing the negative consequences of not solving it.
- **Solve**: Present your product or service as the solution that solves the problem and alleviates the pain.

3. FAB (Features, Advantages, Benefits)

The FAB formula is designed to help you shift from talking about product features to emphasizing the benefits those features provide.

- **Features**: Highlight the features of your product or service.
- **Advantages**: Explain the advantages these features provide over competitors.

- **Benefits**: Focus on the tangible benefits that your audience will experience as a result.

Key Takeaway:

Using proven copywriting frameworks like AIDA, PAS, and FAB can streamline your writing process and guide your audience toward conversion. These frameworks ensure that your message is structured in a way that captures attention, builds interest, and leads to action.

4: Crafting Headlines That Convert

Your headline is the first (and sometimes only) thing a potential customer will read. If your headline doesn't grab attention, the rest of your copy may never be seen. Crafting compelling headlines is critical to the success of your marketing efforts.

What Makes a Great Headline?

A great headline has three key characteristics:

- **Clear**: It clearly conveys the value or benefit of your offer.
- **Specific**: It provides specific details that pique curiosity or interest.
- **Benefit-focused**: It highlights the main benefit that the reader will gain from engaging with your content.

Proven Headline Formulas

1. **The "How to" Headline**

- Example: "How to Lose 10 Pounds in 30 Days Without Giving Up Your Favorite Foods"

2. Why it works: It promises a clear, specific outcome and provides a solution to a common problem.
3. **The Question Headline**
   - Example: "Are You Making These Common SEO Mistakes?"
4. Why it works: It engages the reader by asking a question that relates to their pain points or challenges, prompting them to seek the answer.
5. **The List Headline**
   - Example: "7 Proven Ways to Boost Your Website Traffic Overnight"
6. Why it works: People love lists because they promise quick, digestible information.
7. **The Benefit-Driven Headline**
   - Example: "Discover the Secret to Doubling Your Sales in 90 Days"
8. Why it works: It focuses on the benefit the reader will gain, making it hard to ignore.
9. **The Urgency Headline**
   - Example: "Limited Time Offer: Get 50% Off Your First Purchase—Ends Tonight!"
10. Why it works: It creates urgency, encouraging the reader to act immediately.

Key Takeaway:

Headlines are critical to grabbing attention and driving clicks. By using proven headline formulas that are clear, specific, and benefit-driven, you can significantly increase engagement and conversions.

5: Writing Strong Calls to Action (CTAs)

A well-crafted call to action (CTA) is what turns interested readers into paying customers. Your CTA should be clear, specific, and designed to inspire immediate action.

What Makes a CTA Effective?

An effective CTA is:

- **Clear**: It tells the reader exactly what to do next (e.g., "Buy Now," "Sign Up Today").
- **Urgent**: It encourages the reader to act quickly by creating a sense of urgency (e.g., "Limited Spots Available," "Offer Ends Tonight").
- **Benefit-driven**: It emphasizes what the reader will gain by taking action (e.g., "Get Your Free Guide Now").

CTA Placement

Your CTA should be strategically placed where it's most likely to capture attention. Common placement options include:

- **At the end of your copy**: After you've explained the value of your offer, place the CTA at the end to drive action.
- **In the middle of your copy**: For longer-form copy, place CTAs throughout to capture readers who may be ready to act before reaching the end.
- **In pop-ups or banners**: Eye-catching pop-ups or banners with a strong CTA can capture attention at key moments, such as when a visitor is about to leave your site.

Key Takeaway:

Your CTA is the critical final step in converting readers into customers. Make it clear, benefit-driven, and urgent to inspire immediate action.

Conclusion: Turning Words Into Sales

Compelling copy is the backbone of successful marketing. By understanding your audience, leveraging psychological triggers, using proven copywriting frameworks, and crafting attention-grabbing headlines and calls to action, you can create copy that not only engages but converts.

Remember, great copy doesn't happen by accident—it requires a deep understanding of your audience's needs, desires, and pain points, and a strategic approach to guiding them through the buying journey.

Chapter 9

REAL-WORLD CASE STUDIES OF IRRESISTIBLE OFFERS IN DIGITAL MARKETING

The power of an irresistible offer in digital marketing is undeniable. Whether you're selling physical products, digital goods, or services, crafting an offer that your audience finds irresistible can make the difference between a campaign's success and failure. But what does it take to create such an offer, and how can you replicate that success?

This chapter will delve into real-world case studies of brands and businesses that have created and executed irresistible offers in digital marketing. We'll explore what made these offers so effective, break down the strategies behind them, and identify the key takeaways that you can apply to your own campaigns.

1: ClickFunnels' "One Funnel Away" Challenge

Overview

ClickFunnels, the popular sales funnel software company founded by Russell Brunson, created one of the most successful digital marketing offers with its **"One Funnel Away Challenge"**. This offer is designed to help entrepreneurs build a fully functioning sales funnel in 30 days, even if they've never built one before.

The Offer

The One Funnel Away (OFA) Challenge was positioned as an intense 30-day training program for entrepreneurs who wanted to master online sales funnels. For a low entry price of $100, participants received:

- Daily video coaching and training from Russell Brunson, Julie Stoian, and Stephen Larsen.
- Worksheets, homework assignments, and templates to help them build their funnel.
- Access to a private Facebook group for support and accountability.
- The **30 Days eBook**, where 30 entrepreneurs outlined what they would do if they had to start from scratch.

In addition to these core elements, ClickFunnels layered in several bonuses, including access to the **30-Day Summit**, where participants could hear from experts who had built successful businesses using ClickFunnels.

Why It Was Irresistible

1. **Clear and Specific Promise**: The offer promised a specific outcome—building a sales funnel in 30 days. This clear, achievable goal attracted entrepreneurs looking for a structured solution.

2. **Low Cost for High Value**: The entry price of $100 was incredibly low for the amount of value delivered. The inclusion of expert coaching, templates, and bonuses made the offer feel like an easy decision.
3. **Community and Accountability**: Participants were given access to a private Facebook group where they could interact with other like-minded entrepreneurs. This sense of community, combined with accountability, made the offer even more appealing.
4. **Risk-Free Upsell**: ClickFunnels effectively used the OFA Challenge as a low-cost entry point for its core product, the ClickFunnels software. Many participants eventually upgraded to the software after seeing the value in the challenge.

Results and Takeaways

The One Funnel Away Challenge was a massive success, generating millions in revenue for ClickFunnels and introducing countless new users to the platform. It also created a highly engaged community of users who became advocates for the brand.

Key Takeaway: Offer a clear, specific transformation at a low price point, then overdeliver with bonuses and community support. If possible, use the offer as a low-risk entry point to introduce prospects to higher-ticket products or services.

2: Dollar Shave Club's Disruptive Subscription Model

Overview

Dollar Shave Club (DSC) launched with a simple yet highly effective value proposition: quality razors delivered to your door for just $1 per month. This disruptive subscription model quickly took off, turning DSC into a billion-dollar company.

The Offer

Dollar Shave Club's irresistible offer centered around simplicity and affordability. For just $1, customers could get their first month of razors, and thereafter, they could choose between three different subscription levels:

- The **Humble Twin**: $1 per month for two blades.
- The **4X**: $6 per month for four blades.
- The **Executive**: $9 per month for six blades.

The offer also included free shipping and the option to cancel anytime, which added to its appeal.

Why It Was Irresistible

1. **Price Disruption**: At a time when men were paying $20 or more for razors at retail stores, Dollar Shave Club's offer of razors for $1/month was a game-changer. The dramatically lower price attracted attention and positioned DSC as a cost-effective alternative to traditional razor brands.

2. **Convenience**: The subscription model made shaving easy and hassle-free. Customers no longer had to go to the store to buy razors—they were delivered right to their door.
3. **Engaging Marketing**: DSC's viral launch video, featuring the company's CEO, Michael Dubin, humorously explaining the offer, was an integral part of the campaign's success. The video generated millions of views, helping to spread the word about the offer and attract customers.
4. **No-Risk Trial**: The $1 first-month offer allowed customers to try the service with very little risk. The low price point and free shipping made it easy for customers to justify trying the product.

Results and Takeaways

Dollar Shave Club's $1 offer helped the company acquire thousands of customers quickly. Their success eventually led to a $1 billion acquisition by Unilever in 2016. The key was a combination of disruptive pricing, convenience, and humorous, relatable marketing.

Key Takeaway: If you can offer a product at a disruptive price point, combine it with convenience and risk-free trials to capture your market's attention. Effective branding and marketing can amplify the impact of a simple, compelling offer.

3: Shopify's 14-Day Free Trial

Overview

Shopify, a leading e-commerce platform, has built a multi-billion-dollar business by helping entrepreneurs create and run online stores. A key component of their success has been their irresistible offer: a **14-day free trial** that lets users explore the platform risk-free before committing to a paid plan.

The Offer

Shopify's free trial offer gives users access to all the essential tools and features they need to start building their e-commerce store. During the 14-day period, users can:

- Set up their store and add products.
- Customize their website with themes and branding.
- Process orders, payments, and shipping.
- Access customer support and educational resources.

Once the trial ends, users can choose from several paid plans starting at $29 per month.

Why It Was Irresistible

1. **Risk-Free Trial**: Shopify's free trial allowed users to experience the full functionality of the platform without having to commit to a paid plan. This eliminated any financial risk, making it easier for potential customers to give Shopify a try.
2. **Full Access**: Unlike limited trials, Shopify provided full access to their platform, giving users a complete experience of what it would be like to run an online store with Shopify. This allowed potential customers to fully test the platform and see how it met their needs.
3. **Onboarding and Support**: During the trial period, Shopify provided users with comprehensive

onboarding materials, tutorials, and customer support. This ensured that new users had the guidance they needed to succeed and increased the likelihood of converting trial users into paying customers.

4. **Low Barrier to Entry**: Shopify's monthly pricing plans are relatively low, starting at $29/month. This low barrier to entry, combined with the free trial, made it an attractive option for entrepreneurs looking to start an online business.

Results and Takeaways

Shopify's 14-day free trial offer has been instrumental in its growth. The platform now powers over 1 million businesses globally, generating billions in revenue. By offering a risk-free entry point, Shopify effectively built trust with potential customers and allowed them to experience the platform's value firsthand.

Key Takeaway: Offering a free trial that provides full access to your product or service is an effective way to reduce risk and encourage prospects to try your offer. Support your free trial with excellent onboarding and educational resources to ensure users get the most out of their experience.

4: Amazon Prime's Membership Offer

Overview

Amazon Prime, the subscription service offered by Amazon, is one of the most successful membership programs in history. Prime provides members with a range of benefits, including free two-day shipping, access to streaming video and music, exclusive deals, and more. The key to its success? An irresistible 30-day free trial that hooks customers in before asking them to commit.

The Offer

Amazon Prime's initial offer allows users to try the service for 30 days for free. During this trial period, customers enjoy all the benefits of Prime, including:

- Free two-day shipping on eligible items.
- Access to Prime Video, with thousands of TV shows and movies.
- Prime Music streaming service.
- Prime Reading, offering access to a vast library of books and magazines.
- Exclusive deals on products and services.

After the 30-day trial, customers are billed at $12.99/ month or $119/year, depending on the plan they choose.

Why It Was Irresistible

1. **High Perceived Value**: The range of benefits included in the Prime membership offers incredible value for a relatively low price. The free trial allowed customers to experience the full benefits of Prime without any financial commitment, making it easy to see the value.
2. **Multiple Touchpoints**: Prime's benefits extend across several areas, including entertainment, shopping, and reading. This ensures that there is

something for everyone, increasing the likelihood that customers will find value in the service.

3. **Convenience**: Free two-day shipping is one of the most significant benefits of Prime, and it appeals to Amazon's massive base of frequent shoppers. The convenience of fast, free shipping adds to the appeal of the offer.
4. **Built-In Retention**: Once users experience the benefits of Prime, they are more likely to continue with the service after the trial period ends. Amazon's subscription model, combined with the convenience and value of Prime, leads to high retention rates.

Results and Takeaways

Amazon Prime has grown to over 200 million members worldwide, and the 30-day free trial offer has played a significant role in that growth. The free trial makes it easy for customers to try Prime without risk, and the extensive benefits make it hard for them to cancel once they've experienced it.

Key Takeaway: Offering a free trial for a membership service with high perceived value and multiple benefits is a powerful way to attract and retain customers. When customers experience the value firsthand, they're more likely to continue with the service long term.

5: The Tim Ferriss Book Launches

Overview

Tim Ferriss, author of best-selling books such as **The 4-Hour Workweek**, **The 4-Hour Body**, and **Tools of Titans**, has mastered the art of creating irresistible offers around his book launches. Ferriss' marketing strategy combines bonus offers, social proof, and exclusivity to drive massive book sales and create a loyal audience.

The Offer

For each of his book launches, Ferriss has offered a range of bonuses to incentivize pre-orders and early purchases. For example, during the launch of **Tools of Titans**, Ferriss offered the following:

- **Digital bonuses**: Early buyers received exclusive access to digital content, including audio interviews, behind-the-scenes materials, and bonus chapters.
- **Exclusive webinars**: Those who pre-ordered multiple copies were invited to join private webinars with Ferriss, where they could ask questions and interact with him directly.
- **Limited edition signed copies**: For those who ordered in bulk, Ferriss offered signed copies of the book as well as limited-edition packages that included additional bonuses.

Why It Was Irresistible

1. **Exclusive Bonuses**: The bonuses were tailored specifically to Ferriss' audience, offering them valuable, exclusive content they couldn't get anywhere else. This added value to the pre-order and created a sense of urgency.
2. **Community Engagement**: Ferriss' offers often included direct interaction with him through

webinars or live events, giving his audience a personal connection to the author. This sense of community and exclusivity made the offer even more attractive.

3. **Tiered Incentives**: By offering different bonuses based on the number of books purchased, Ferriss incentivized bulk purchases, driving up his pre-order numbers and increasing his chances of hitting bestseller lists.
4. **Social Proof**: Ferriss' books come with a built-in level of trust, as his audience knows the high quality of his previous work. This, combined with endorsements from notable figures, made his offers even more compelling.

Results and Takeaways

Tim Ferriss' book launches have consistently been hugely successful, with multiple books reaching #1 on The New York Times Bestseller list. By creating irresistible pre-order offers, Ferriss has built a loyal following and maximized sales during his launch periods.

Key Takeaway: Create exclusive, high-value bonuses that resonate with your audience to incentivize pre-orders and early purchases. Offering multiple tiers of incentives can drive bulk purchases and amplify the success of your product launch.

Conclusion: Lessons Learned from Irresistible Offers

The real-world case studies explored in this chapter demonstrate that an irresistible offer is not just about the product or service itself—it's about how you package, position, and market that offer to your audience. Whether through free trials, bonuses, limited-time deals, or innovative pricing models, these businesses have mastered the art of creating offers that people simply can't refuse.

Key Lessons from the Case Studies

1. **Provide Clear Value**: Each of these offers provided clear, tangible value to the customer, whether through cost savings, convenience, or exclusive content. When customers understand exactly what they're getting and how it benefits them, they're more likely to take action.
2. **Reduce Risk**: Risk reversal strategies, such as free trials or money-back guarantees, reduce the perceived risk for the customer, making it easier for them to say "yes" to the offer.
3. **Create Urgency**: Many of the offers created urgency by using scarcity or time-limited deals. This urgency motivated customers to act quickly rather than putting off the decision.
4. **Leverage Social Proof**: Social proof, such as testimonials, reviews, and case studies, played a significant role in building trust and credibility, making the offers more appealing.
5. **Offer Bonuses and Exclusive Access**: Adding bonuses, exclusive content, or early access incentives makes an offer feel more valuable and can encourage customers to take action sooner.

By understanding the strategies behind these irresistible offers, you can apply the same principles to your own digital marketing campaigns. Whether you're selling products, services, or content, the right offer can turn prospects into customers and drive long-term business success.

Chapter 10

COMMON MISTAKES AND PITFALLS TO AVOID WHILE CREATING OFFERS

Creating irresistible offers is a critical component of any successful marketing strategy. However, even the most well-intentioned marketers can fall into common traps that undermine the effectiveness of their offers. These mistakes can lead to missed opportunities, wasted marketing budgets, and, most importantly, lost sales.

In this chapter, we will explore the most frequent mistakes and pitfalls businesses encounter when crafting offers and how to avoid them. By learning from these common errors, you can create offers that not only capture your audience's attention but also drive meaningful action and conversions.

1: Failing to Understand Your Target Audience

The Pitfall

One of the most fundamental mistakes businesses make when creating offers is not understanding their target audience deeply enough. When you don't know who your ideal customer is, it's nearly impossible to craft an offer that resonates with their specific needs, desires, and pain points. Generic offers often fall flat because they don't speak to the motivations or challenges of the people you're trying to reach.

For example, a high-ticket coaching program aimed at corporate professionals will fail if it's marketed the same way as a low-cost fitness app for busy moms. Each audience has different priorities, pain points, and expectations that should be reflected in your offer.

How to Avoid It

To avoid this pitfall, you must develop a clear and detailed understanding of your target audience by creating **buyer personas**. Buyer personas are fictional representations of your ideal customers, based on real data and insights. When creating personas, ask questions like:

- What are their primary challenges or pain points?
- What motivates them to take action or make a purchase?
- What are their core values, and how do they align with your brand?
- What are their objections or concerns about buying?

Once you have a clear picture of your audience, you can tailor your offer to speak directly to their specific needs and desires.

Key Takeaway

Before creating any offer, invest time in deeply understanding your target audience. Offers should be personalized to address their unique problems, desires, and buying behavior.

2: Making Offers Too Complicated

The Pitfall

In an attempt to add as much value as possible, many marketers fall into the trap of making their offers too complicated. They pack their offer with numerous bonuses, features, and options, thinking that more is better. However, this often leads to decision fatigue and confusion for the customer.

A common mistake is offering too many choices at once or overwhelming potential buyers with overly detailed descriptions of product features without clearly highlighting the benefits. Customers faced with complicated offers are more likely to delay making a decision—or worse, abandon the offer entirely.

How to Avoid It

Simplicity is key to creating an offer that converts. A successful offer should be:

- **Clear and straightforward**: Ensure that the value proposition is easy to understand at a glance.
- **Benefit-focused**: Highlight the main benefit or solution your product offers, rather than overwhelming potential buyers with technical details or multiple options.
- **Easy to accept**: The fewer decisions customers need to make, the better. Limit choices to a single

clear action or a small number of variations (e.g., basic, premium, deluxe packages).

If you include bonuses, ensure they are highly relevant to the core offer and clearly explained. Don't add irrelevant extras just for the sake of increasing perceived value.

Key Takeaway

Keep your offers simple and benefit-driven. Avoid overwhelming potential buyers with too many choices, technical jargon, or unnecessary extras.

3: Focusing on Features Instead of Benefits

The Pitfall

Another common mistake is focusing too heavily on the features of your product or service rather than the benefits. While features describe what your product does, benefits explain how it improves the customer's life. Consumers are far more interested in how a product will solve their problem or fulfill their desire than in its technical specifications.

For example, instead of highlighting that a vacuum cleaner has a "5,000 RPM motor" (feature), focus on the fact that it "leaves your floors spotless in half the time" (benefit). Customers want to know how your product will make their life easier, save them time, or help them achieve their goals.

How to Avoid It

To avoid this pitfall, always translate features into benefits. Ask yourself:

- What does this feature do for the customer?
- How will this feature improve their life or solve a specific problem?

When writing copy for your offer, use the **"So what?" test** to ensure you're focusing on the right aspects. For every feature you mention, ask yourself, "So what?" If the answer doesn't clearly articulate a tangible benefit, you need to reframe it in terms of value to the customer.

Key Takeaway

Customers care more about how your product will benefit them than its technical features. Make sure your offer communicates the clear, tangible benefits that your product or service provides.

4: Offering Too Many Discounts or Relying on Price Alone

The Pitfall

While discounts can be an effective way to attract buyers, over-reliance on price cuts can devalue your product and train your audience to wait for deals. Offering too many discounts can also lead to lower profit margins and create a perception that your product isn't worth its full price. Furthermore, discounts alone don't create lasting loyalty or differentiation from competitors who can easily match or undercut your prices.

Many marketers mistakenly believe that lowering the price is the only way to make an offer more attractive. In reality, focusing solely on price can commoditize your product, making it harder to stand out based on value.

How to Avoid It

Instead of focusing on price cuts, focus on **adding value** to your offer. This can be achieved through:

- **Exclusive bonuses**: Offer additional products or services that complement the main offer.
- **Enhanced customer experience**: Provide superior customer support, faster delivery, or personalized services that justify the price.
- **Loyalty programs**: Reward repeat customers with exclusive perks, discounts, or early access to new products.

If you do offer discounts, use them strategically. For example, offering a limited-time discount during a product launch or holiday can create urgency without devaluing your brand. Make sure your discount strategy aligns with your overall business goals and doesn't erode long-term value.

Key Takeaway

Price is not the only lever you can pull to create a compelling offer. Instead of relying solely on discounts, focus on adding value through bonuses, improved customer experiences, or exclusive offers.

5: Lack of Urgency or Scarcity

The Pitfall

One of the most common reasons offers fail to convert is a lack of urgency or scarcity. When customers don't feel any pressure to act immediately, they are likely to postpone their decision or forget about the offer altogether. Without a clear reason to act now, even an attractive offer may sit idle.

Offers that are always available with no end date or that lack any perceived limitation create no motivation for customers to act quickly. They may even devalue the offer by making it seem too accessible.

How to Avoid It

To overcome this pitfall, you need to incorporate elements of **urgency** or **scarcity** into your offer. Some effective strategies include:

- **Limited-time discounts**: Offering a special price or bonus for a limited time encourages customers to take action before the deadline.
- **Limited availability**: If a product or service is available in limited quantities, communicate that clearly (e.g., "Only 10 spots left!").
- **Time-sensitive bonuses**: Offer an exclusive bonus for early buyers or those who purchase within a specific timeframe.

Make sure the urgency or scarcity is genuine. If customers sense that the scarcity is fabricated, it can erode trust in your brand.

Key Takeaway

Create a sense of urgency or scarcity to motivate customers to take action quickly. Limited-time offers, exclusive bonuses, and limited availability can drive immediate conversions.

6: Ignoring Customer Objections

The Pitfall

Every potential customer has objections—reasons why they may hesitate to purchase. These could be concerns about price, trust, product quality, or whether the product will meet their needs. A common mistake is failing to address these objections head-on in your offer. When objections are left unaddressed, customers may abandon the purchase process without taking action.

For example, if a customer is unsure about how your service works or is worried about the commitment, failing to address these concerns could result in a lost sale.

How to Avoid It

To avoid this pitfall, you must proactively identify and address the most common objections your audience might have. Some strategies include:

- **Money-back guarantees**: Offering a refund or satisfaction guarantee removes the risk for the customer.
- **Customer testimonials**: Use social proof to show that other customers have had positive experiences with your product or service.

- **FAQs**: Include a well-crafted FAQ section that addresses common concerns or questions, such as shipping times, returns, or product functionality.

When addressing objections, don't be defensive. Instead, frame your responses in a way that reassures the customer and builds trust.

Key Takeaway

Address customer objections directly in your offer. Money-back guarantees, testimonials, and FAQs can help alleviate concerns and increase conversions.

7: Neglecting to Include a Clear Call to Action

The Pitfall

Even if you've created a great offer, it won't convert if you fail to include a clear and compelling **call to action (CTA)**. A common mistake is assuming that the customer will know what to do next without being explicitly told. In reality, customers need clear guidance on the exact steps they should take to claim the offer.

A vague or weak CTA can result in confusion or inaction. For example, a CTA like "Learn More" is less effective than "Get Your Free Trial Now" because it lacks a sense of urgency or clarity.

How to Avoid It

To avoid this pitfall, ensure that your CTA is:

- **Clear and specific**: Tell the customer exactly what to do (e.g., "Sign up now," "Download today").

- **Action-oriented**: Use action verbs that prompt immediate action, such as "Get started," "Claim your discount," or "Buy now."
- **Benefit-driven**: Reinforce the value of the offer in the CTA (e.g., "Get your free guide now and start saving today").

Also, make sure your CTA is highly visible and easy to find. Place it prominently in your sales page, emails, or advertisements, and use contrasting colors or bold fonts to make it stand out.

Key Takeaway

A strong call to action is essential to converting prospects. Ensure your CTA is clear, action-oriented, and reinforces the value of your offer.

Conclusion: Crafting Offers That Convert

Creating an irresistible offer requires more than just putting together a promotion or discount. It involves understanding your audience, simplifying your message, focusing on value, and addressing customer objections and motivations. The common mistakes outlined in this chapter—from failing to understand your audience to neglecting urgency and clarity—can hinder your success if not addressed.

Final Key Takeaways:

1. **Know Your Audience**: Craft your offer to speak directly to the specific needs, pain points, and desires

of your target audience. Without this understanding, even the best-crafted offer will struggle to resonate.

2. **Keep It Simple**: Avoid overwhelming your prospects with complex choices, features, or messaging. The clearer and more straightforward your offer, the easier it will be for customers to say "yes."
3. **Focus on Benefits, Not Features**: Customers care about how your product or service will solve their problems or improve their lives. Always lead with the benefits that matter most to your audience.
4. **Don't Over-Rely on Discounts**: While discounts can be effective, relying on them too heavily can damage your brand's perceived value. Focus on adding value instead.
5. **Create Urgency**: Incorporate urgency or scarcity to motivate customers to act quickly. A sense of urgency helps overcome hesitation and drives conversions.
6. **Address Objections**: Proactively address customer objections by offering guarantees, showcasing testimonials, and providing clear, detailed information.
7. **Use a Strong Call to Action**: Your CTA should be clear, action-oriented, and reinforce the benefits of the offer. Make sure it's easy for customers to understand what to do next.

By avoiding these common pitfalls and following best practices, you can create offers that not only capture attention but also convert prospects into loyal customers. Crafting the perfect offer is both an art and a science, and by learning from mistakes, you'll be better equipped to create compelling offers that drive success in your digital marketing efforts.

Chapter 11

TESTING, REFINING, AND OPTIMIZING YOUR OFFER

Creating an irresistible offer is only half the battle in digital marketing. Once you've crafted what you believe is a compelling proposition, the real work begins: testing, refining, and optimizing that offer to ensure it converts at the highest possible rate. Offers that perform well initially may still have room for improvement, while others may require significant adjustments to meet your audience's needs and expectations.

In this chapter, we'll explore the importance of systematically testing and refining your offer to maximize its effectiveness. We will discuss various methods for testing, how to analyze the data you collect, and strategies for optimizing your offer based on real-world results. By the end, you'll have a clear roadmap for continuously improving your offers to drive conversions and revenue.

1: The Importance of Testing Offers

Why Testing is Crucial

Testing is one of the most important components of creating an effective offer in digital marketing. Even the most well-crafted offer can fall short if it doesn't resonate with your audience, or if there are hidden barriers that prevent customers from converting. The only way to truly understand how your offer performs is to test it in real-world conditions and use data to guide your decision-making.

Without testing, you're making assumptions about what will work for your audience, which can lead to missed opportunities and wasted resources. Testing allows you to:

- **Identify weak points**: Uncover specific areas in your offer where potential customers drop off or lose interest.
- **Discover what resonates**: Find out which elements of your offer are most appealing and which fall flat.
- **Improve conversion rates**: Systematically increase conversions by refining the elements of your offer that directly impact buying behavior.

Types of Testing in Digital Marketing

There are several types of testing that marketers use to optimize offers. The two most common are **A/B testing** and **multivariate testing**.

A/B Testing

A/B testing, also known as split testing, is a method in which two versions of an offer are presented to different segments of your audience to determine which version performs better. For example, you might test two different headlines on a landing page or two versions of a call to action in an email. By comparing performance metrics, such as click-through rates or conversions, you can determine which version of the offer is more effective.

Example:

You're promoting a new eBook. You decide to A/B test two landing page headlines:

- Version A: "Get Your Free eBook and Boost Your Marketing Today!"
- Version B: "Download Our Expert Guide to Marketing Success—Free for a Limited Time!"

By tracking which headline results in more downloads, you can determine which one resonates more with your audience and refine your offer accordingly.

Multivariate Testing

Multivariate testing takes A/B testing a step further by allowing you to test multiple elements of your offer simultaneously. This method is more complex but can provide deeper insights into how different components of your offer interact with one another. For example, you could test different combinations of headlines, imagery, and call-to-action buttons to see which combination yields the highest conversion rate.

Example:

You're testing a landing page that promotes an online course. With multivariate testing, you could test the following elements at once:

- Three different headlines.
- Two different images.
- Two different call-to-action buttons.

By testing all of these variables together, you can identify the combination that performs best, giving you a fully optimized landing page.

How to Choose What to Test

Before you begin testing, it's important to prioritize what elements of your offer to test first. Focus on elements that are likely to have the biggest impact on conversions. These typically include:

- **Headline**: The headline is often the first thing a visitor sees, and it has a significant impact on whether they continue engaging with your offer.
- **Call to Action (CTA)**: The clarity and urgency of your CTA can make or break conversions.
- **Pricing**: Small changes in pricing or pricing structure can have a major impact on buyer behavior.
- **Offer details**: Elements like bonuses, guarantees, or limited-time offers can influence how compelling your offer is.
- **Visuals**: Images, videos, and overall page design play a key role in how your offer is perceived.

Key Takeaway:

Testing is critical to optimizing your offer. By systematically testing different components, you can identify what works and what doesn't, leading to more effective offers that drive higher conversion rates.

2: Setting Up and Executing A/B Tests

The A/B Testing Process

A/B testing is one of the simplest and most effective ways to optimize your offer. However, to get meaningful results, you need to follow a structured process. Here's how to set up and execute an A/B test:

Step 1: Define Your Objective

Before you begin your test, it's essential to clearly define your objective. What are you trying to achieve? Your goal could be to increase the click-through rate on a call-to-action button, boost conversion rates on a landing page, or reduce cart abandonment.

For example, if your goal is to increase the number of visitors who sign up for a free trial, your objective is to improve the conversion rate of the sign-up page.

Step 2: Choose a Variable to Test

Next, choose the specific variable you want to test. Remember, A/B testing works best when you test one variable at a time. Some common variables to test include:

- **Headline**: Does a benefit-focused headline perform better than a curiosity-driven headline?
- **Call to Action**: Does "Start Your Free Trial" perform better than "Sign Up Now"?
- **Button Color**: Does a green "Buy Now" button get more clicks than a red one?
- **Pricing**: Does offering a payment plan increase conversions?

Step 3: Create Two Versions (A and B)

Once you've chosen your variable, create two versions of your offer: Version A (the control) and Version B (the variant). Make sure that both versions are identical except for the one variable you are testing. This ensures that any difference in performance can be attributed to the variable you are testing.

For example, if you're testing a headline, Version A might have a direct headline ("Sign Up for Our Free Course Today"), while Version B might have a curiosity-driven headline ("Ready to Learn a Secret Strategy for Growing Your Business?").

Step 4: Split Your Traffic Evenly

To conduct a proper A/B test, you need to split your traffic evenly between Version A and Version B. This can be done using A/B testing software, which will automatically divide visitors between the two versions.

Step 5: Measure the Results

Let the test run until you've collected enough data to make a statistically significant decision. The length of time needed depends on your traffic volume. For most tests, you should aim to have at least 100 conversions per variation to ensure reliable results.

Analyze the performance of each version based on the metric you're tracking (e.g., conversion rate, click-through rate). The version with the better performance is your winner.

Step 6: Implement the Winning Version

Once you've determined the winner, implement the winning version as the new control. From there, you can continue testing other variables to further optimize your offer.

Common Mistakes in A/B Testing

- **Ending Tests Too Early**: One of the most common mistakes is ending a test before enough data has been collected. Be patient and allow the test to run until it reaches statistical significance.
- **Testing Too Many Variables at Once**: A/B testing should focus on a single variable. Testing multiple variables simultaneously can lead to confusing results.
- **Not Defining a Clear Objective**: Without a clear goal, it's hard to know what success looks like. Always define your objective before starting a test.

Key Takeaway:

A/B testing is a powerful tool for refining your offer. By focusing on one variable at a time and allowing the test to run long enough to collect significant data, you can make informed decisions that lead to higher conversions.

3: Using Multivariate Testing to Optimize Complex Offers

What is Multivariate Testing?

While A/B testing is ideal for testing one element at a time, **multivariate testing** allows you to test multiple elements simultaneously to determine which combination of changes produces the best results. This method is particularly useful when you have a complex offer with multiple variables that could impact conversion rates.

For example, if you're running a landing page for a product launch, you might want to test several variations of the headline, CTA, and images. With multivariate testing, you can test all these elements together to find the most effective combination.

When to Use Multivariate Testing

Multivariate testing is best used when you have a significant amount of traffic and want to test multiple variables at once. It's especially helpful for optimizing complex offers, such as:

- **Landing pages**: If your landing page has multiple elements that influence conversions (e.g., headline, CTA, images, testimonials), multivariate testing allows you to optimize them in parallel.
- **Email marketing**: You can test subject lines, email copy, CTA buttons, and design elements to find the most effective combination.
- **Ad campaigns**: If you're running ads on multiple platforms (e.g., Facebook, Google), you can use multivariate testing to optimize everything from ad copy to visuals.

How Multivariate Testing Works

In multivariate testing, you create multiple variations of each element you want to test. The testing software will then create different combinations of these elements and show them to your audience. Here's an example:

Let's say you're testing three elements on a landing page:

- **Headline**: You create two variations (Version A and Version B).
- **CTA Button**: You create two variations (Version A and Version B).
- **Image**: You create two variations (Version A and Version B).

The testing software will automatically generate four different combinations:

1. Headline A + CTA Button A + Image A.
2. Headline A + CTA Button B + Image B.
3. Headline B + CTA Button A + Image B.
4. Headline B + CTA Button B + Image A.

Each combination will be shown to a portion of your audience, and you can track which combination produces the highest conversion rate.

Benefits of Multivariate Testing

- **More Data**: Multivariate testing provides deeper insights because it shows you how different elements work together. You can identify the combination of elements that produces the best overall result.
- **Faster Optimization**: Since you're testing multiple variables at once, you can optimize your offer

more quickly than if you were testing each element individually.

Challenges of Multivariate Testing

- **Requires High Traffic**: Because multivariate testing involves testing multiple combinations, you need a large amount of traffic to generate statistically significant results.
- **Complexity**: Multivariate testing is more complex to set up and analyze than A/B testing, so it's important to have the right tools and expertise in place.

Key Takeaway:

Multivariate testing is an advanced technique that allows you to optimize multiple elements of your offer simultaneously. While it requires more traffic and complexity, it provides deeper insights into what combinations drive the highest conversions.

4: Analyzing Test Results and Identifying Patterns

How to Analyze Your Test Results

Once you've completed your A/B or multivariate test, it's time to analyze the data. The key is to look beyond the raw numbers and identify the underlying patterns that explain why one version of your offer outperformed the other. Here's a step-by-step process for analyzing your test results:

Step 1: Compare Key Metrics

Start by comparing the key metrics that align with your objectives. Depending on your goal, this could include:

- **Conversion Rate**: The percentage of visitors who completed the desired action (e.g., made a purchase, signed up for a free trial).
- **Click-Through Rate (CTR)**: The percentage of people who clicked on a CTA or ad.
- **Bounce Rate**: The percentage of visitors who leave your page without taking action.
- **Time on Page**: How long visitors spend on your page.

For example, if your goal was to increase conversions on a landing page, you would focus primarily on the conversion rate.

Step 2: Look for Statistically Significant Results

To ensure that your test results are reliable, it's important to confirm that the difference in performance between Version A and Version B is statistically significant. Statistical significance means that the difference is not due to random chance but is a true reflection of how the variations performed.

Most A/B testing software includes a statistical significance calculator that will tell you whether your results are significant. A common threshold is 95%, meaning there's only a 5% chance that the difference is due to random variation.

Step 3: Identify Trends and Patterns

Once you've determined which version performed better, dig deeper into the data to understand why. Look for trends and patterns that could explain the difference in performance. For example:

- Did Version B have a higher conversion rate because the headline was more benefit-focused?
- Did visitors spend more time on Version A because the design was more engaging?
- Did the bounce rate decrease on Version B because the offer was clearer and more compelling?

By identifying these patterns, you can gain valuable insights into what resonates with your audience and what areas need improvement.

Step 4: Segment Your Audience

It's also helpful to segment your audience and analyze how different groups responded to the test. For example, you might find that one version of your offer performed better with mobile users, while another version resonated more with desktop users.

Other common segments to analyze include:

- **New vs. returning visitors**: Are repeat visitors more likely to convert on a specific version?
- **Geographic location**: Do users from different regions respond differently to the offer?
- **Demographics**: Does the offer resonate more with a specific age group or gender?

By analyzing different segments, you can tailor future offers to specific audience groups and further optimize your overall strategy.

Avoiding False Positives

When analyzing test results, it's important to avoid false positives—results that appear significant but are actually due to random chance. To avoid false positives:

- **Run tests long enough**: Ensure your test has collected enough data to be statistically significant. Don't end tests prematurely based on early results.
- **Use a significance calculator**: Confirm that your results meet the threshold for statistical significance (usually 95%).

Key Takeaway:

Analyzing your test results is crucial for identifying what's working and what needs improvement. Look for patterns and trends in the data, and segment your audience to gain deeper insights into how different groups respond to your offer.

5: Refining Your Offer Based on Test Results

Using Data to Make Informed Decisions

Once you've analyzed your test results and identified the winning version of your offer, it's time to refine your offer based on the insights you've gathered. This process of **iterative optimization** is key to creating offers that consistently perform at the highest level.

The goal of refining your offer is to make data-driven decisions that improve key metrics such as conversion rates, customer satisfaction, and overall revenue. Here's how to approach the refinement process:

Step 1: Apply the Winning Elements

The first step is to implement the elements of your offer that performed best in the test. This might include:

- Using the headline that generated the highest conversion rate.
- Keeping the CTA that drove the most clicks.
- Highlighting the pricing model that produced the most sales.

By applying these winning elements, you ensure that your offer is optimized based on real-world data rather than assumptions.

Step 2: Address Weak Points

While testing reveals what works, it also uncovers weak points that may be holding back the effectiveness of your offer. For example, if the test results showed that your bounce rate was still high, it could indicate that visitors are not fully engaged with your page or are confused by the offer.

To address weak points, ask yourself:

- Is the offer clearly communicated?
- Are there any distractions or barriers preventing customers from converting?
- Are the benefits of the offer emphasized strongly enough?

Refine the weak areas based on the feedback and data you've gathered, and consider running additional tests to validate these changes.

Step 3: Iterate and Test Again

Optimization is an ongoing process. Once you've refined your offer, it's important to continue testing new variations to further improve performance. Each test provides new insights that can lead to incremental gains in conversion rates and customer satisfaction.

Consider testing:

- **New headlines or messaging**: Even if your headline performed well, there may still be room for improvement.
- **Different bonuses or value propositions**: Test different incentives to see which ones resonate most with your audience.
- **Alternate pricing structures**: Experiment with subscription plans, one-time offers, or tiered pricing to find the most appealing option for your customers.

Step 4: Gather Qualitative Feedback

In addition to quantitative data, qualitative feedback from customers can provide valuable insights into how to refine your offer. Conduct surveys, interviews, or focus groups to gather feedback on:

- What they liked or didn't like about the offer.
- What objections they had before purchasing.
- How they felt about the overall value of the offer.

This feedback can reveal hidden issues that quantitative data alone may not uncover, such as confusion over the offer details or unmet expectations.

Case Study: Refining Based on Customer Feedback

Example: Dropbox

Dropbox, the cloud storage company, initially struggled with low conversion rates during its early days. After conducting user interviews, the team discovered that potential customers were hesitant because they didn't fully understand how Dropbox worked. In response, Dropbox created an explainer video that clearly demonstrated the product's features and benefits. The video was placed prominently on their homepage and led to a significant increase in conversions.

Step 5: Measure Long-Term Impact

As you refine your offer, it's important to track the long-term impact of your changes. While some optimizations may lead to immediate gains, others may take time to show results. For example, changes that improve customer retention or lifetime value may not be immediately visible but can have a significant long-term impact on revenue.

Key Takeaway:

Refining your offer is an ongoing process that requires data-driven decision-making and continuous testing. By applying winning elements, addressing weak points, and gathering both quantitative and qualitative feedback, you can create an offer that consistently performs at a high level.

6: Optimizing Your Offer Across Multiple Channels

Adapting Your Offer for Different Platforms

In today's multi-channel marketing landscape, it's essential to optimize your offer for different platforms and channels. What works on your website's landing page may not perform as well on social media, email, or paid advertising. To maximize the reach and effectiveness of your offer, you need to tailor it for each channel.

Channel 1: Website and Landing Pages

Your website or landing page is often the first point of contact for potential customers. To optimize your offer on these platforms:

- **Use Clear, Compelling Headlines**: The headline should immediately communicate the value of your offer and grab the visitor's attention.
- **Simplify the Offer**: Avoid clutter and distractions. Keep the design clean, with a clear CTA that guides the visitor toward conversion.
- **Use Visuals to Support the Offer**: Images, videos, and graphics

Chapter 12

THE POWER OF REPETITION IN MARKETING

Repetition is a foundational principle in marketing. While creativity and innovation are important, the power of repetition is what solidifies brand recognition, ingrains messages in the minds of consumers, and ultimately drives conversions. Successful brands understand that consistency and repetition across different channels are key to creating lasting impressions and encouraging customer action.

This chapter explores the psychology behind repetition in marketing, the various ways repetition can be used effectively, and how to balance it with creativity and freshness to avoid fatigue. We'll look at real-world examples and best practices that illustrate why repetition remains one of the most powerful tools in a marketer's toolkit.

1: The Psychology of Repetition

Why Repetition Works

Repetition works because it takes advantage of how the human brain processes information. The more we are exposed to a piece of information, the more likely it is that it will be retained in our memory. This is known as the **"mere exposure effect,"** a psychological phenomenon where people tend to develop a preference for things they see or hear repeatedly. In marketing, repetition helps build familiarity and trust, which are critical components of consumer decision-making.

There are several key psychological reasons why repetition is effective:

- **Memory retention**: Our brains are wired to forget information that is only encountered once or twice. Repetition increases the chances that a brand or message will be remembered.
- **Familiarity breeds comfort**: When consumers are repeatedly exposed to a brand or message, it feels more familiar, and they are more likely to trust it. Familiarity reduces perceived risk, which can be a powerful driver in purchasing decisions.
- **Association and recognition**: Repetition creates strong associations between a brand and its messaging, which helps with recall. When a consumer sees or hears a message multiple times, they begin to associate the brand with the benefits or emotions conveyed in the message.

The Learning Curve and Advertising Frequency

The **Ebbinghaus Forgetting Curve** suggests that people forget information over time unless they are exposed to it repeatedly. In advertising, this means that a consumer might need to see an ad several times before the message sticks. According to some marketing studies, it can take anywhere from **7 to 20 exposures** to a message before a consumer makes a purchasing decision.

Repetition also helps consumers progress through the stages of the **buyer's journey**:

1. **Awareness**: At first, consumers are just becoming aware of your brand. The initial exposures might not lead to immediate action, but they plant the seed of recognition.
2. **Consideration**: As consumers see your message more often, they move into the consideration phase, where they start to compare your offer with alternatives.
3. **Decision**: Finally, after repeated exposure, consumers are more likely to choose your product or service because it feels familiar and trustworthy.

Key Takeaway:

Repetition is powerful because it leverages human psychology. It helps improve memory retention, builds familiarity and trust, and guides consumers through the stages of the buyer's journey. Repetition is essential for creating long-term brand recognition.

2: Repetition in Branding and Messaging

Consistency in Branding

In marketing, consistency is closely tied to repetition. Every time a consumer interacts with your brand, they should experience the same core message, values, and visual identity. This consistency reinforces brand recognition and helps create a cohesive image in the minds of your audience.

Brands that are inconsistent in their messaging—using different taglines, visual styles, or tones—risk confusing their audience and diluting the power of their message. Repetition ensures that each interaction with your brand reinforces the same core identity.

Repetition of Brand Elements

Successful brands repeat several core elements to solidify their identity:

- **Logos**: Repetition of a logo helps solidify brand recognition. Think of iconic logos like the Nike swoosh or the McDonald's golden arches. These logos are consistently repeated across every touchpoint, from TV ads to packaging to social media posts.
- **Taglines**: Memorable taglines stick in the mind because they are used repeatedly. Nike's "Just Do It" and Apple's "Think Different" are examples of taglines that have become synonymous with their respective brands due to consistent repetition.
- **Color schemes**: Repetition of brand colors also plays a significant role in recognition. The red and yellow of McDonald's or the blue of Facebook are instantly recognizable because they are consistently repeated across all brand materials.
- **Slogans and messaging**: Repeating key messaging points—such as your brand's unique

value proposition or benefits—helps establish your brand's position in the market.

How Repetition Builds Trust

One of the most significant benefits of repetition is that it builds trust. Consumers are more likely to trust a brand they've encountered multiple times. This is especially important for new or lesser-known brands that need to build credibility. Repetition signals to consumers that the brand is established, reliable, and worth their attention.

Consistency in branding also fosters loyalty. When consumers know what to expect from a brand, they are more likely to become repeat customers. Repeating the same messages and visuals creates a sense of familiarity that strengthens the relationship between the brand and its customers.

Key Takeaway:

Repetition in branding—through consistent use of logos, taglines, colors, and messaging—helps create a cohesive and recognizable brand identity. This repetition builds trust, fosters brand loyalty, and makes it easier for consumers to recognize and remember your brand.

3: Repetition in Advertising Campaigns

The Role of Frequency in Advertising

In advertising, the concept of **frequency** refers to the number of times a consumer is exposed to an ad. While a single exposure to an ad rarely leads to action, repeated exposures increase the likelihood that the consumer will remember the ad and take action.

However, there's a balance to be struck—too little repetition can lead to poor recall, while too much repetition can result in **ad fatigue**, where consumers become annoyed or bored with seeing the same ad over and over again. The goal is to find the optimal frequency that reinforces your message without overwhelming your audience.

Best Practices for Repeating Ads

1. **Vary the Presentation**: While the core message should remain consistent, you can repeat the message in different formats or variations to keep it fresh. For example, a brand could run a series of TV ads that use the same tagline but feature different scenarios or storylines. This repetition with variation helps prevent ad fatigue while still reinforcing the message.
2. **Cross-Channel Consistency**: Repetition across multiple channels increases the chances that your audience will encounter your message in different contexts. A consumer might see your ad on social media, encounter a banner ad on a website, and later hear about your brand in a podcast ad. Each exposure reinforces the previous ones, helping to cement your message in their mind.
3. **Retargeting**: Retargeting is a powerful way to use repetition in digital advertising. By showing ads to people who have already interacted with your

brand—such as visiting your website or adding items to their cart—you increase the chances of conversion. Retargeting leverages repetition by reminding potential customers about your brand and nudging them toward completing a purchase.

4. **Sequential Advertising**: Instead of showing the same ad repeatedly, you can use **sequential advertising**, where each ad builds on the previous one. This strategy helps maintain engagement while still using repetition to reinforce key messages. For example, the first ad might introduce the product, the second ad explains its benefits, and the third ad offers a special discount.

Real-World Examples of Repetition in Advertising

1. **Coca-Cola**: Coca-Cola is a master of repetition in advertising. The brand's "Share a Coke" campaign is a great example of how repetition with variation works. In this campaign, Coca-Cola printed people's names on bottles, creating a personalized experience while still repeating the same core message—"Share a Coke." The repetition of the brand's logo, colors, and messaging across billboards, TV ads, and social media created a cohesive and memorable campaign.
2. **Geico**: Geico's long-running slogan, "15 minutes could save you 15% or more on car insurance," is an excellent example of repetition in action. The message is simple, memorable, and repeated in nearly every Geico ad, whether on TV, radio, or online. This consistent repetition has helped Geico

become one of the most recognizable insurance brands in the world.

3. **Apple**: Apple's advertising often uses repetition to reinforce its brand values of simplicity, innovation, and premium quality. The repetition of clean, minimalist visuals, combined with messages about creativity and technological superiority, helps to maintain Apple's positioning as a leader in the tech industry.

Key Takeaway:

In advertising, repetition is essential for building brand recognition and increasing the likelihood of conversions. Using varied presentations, cross-channel consistency, and retargeting can help you maintain engagement while still reinforcing your core message.

4: The Power of Repetition in Content Marketing

Repeating Key Messages in Content Marketing

Content marketing relies heavily on repetition to reinforce key messages and educate consumers over time. Unlike paid advertising, content marketing often requires multiple touchpoints before a consumer is ready to convert. By repeating key themes and messages in your content, you can build familiarity and trust while gradually moving your audience toward action.

For example, if your brand focuses on sustainability, your blog posts, social media content, and videos should consistently reinforce your commitment to sustainability. The more consumers encounter this message, the more likely they are to associate your brand with eco-friendly values.

Content Repurposing and Repetition

One of the most effective ways to use repetition in content marketing is through **content repurposing**. Content repurposing involves taking a single piece of content and adapting it for use across multiple platforms and formats. This allows you to repeat your core message without having to create entirely new content every time.

For example:

- A blog post can be repurposed into a series of social media posts.
- A webinar can be turned into an eBook or whitepaper.
- A podcast episode can be transcribed and turned into a blog post.

This strategy ensures that your message is consistently repeated across channels while also allowing you to reach different segments of your audience.

The Role of SEO and Repetition

In SEO, repetition is essential for building authority and improving rankings. By consistently producing content around key topics or keywords, you signal to search engines that your website is an authoritative source on those subjects. Over time, this repetition helps improve your website's visibility in search results.

For example, a company specializing in digital marketing services might publish multiple blog posts, case studies, and guides that all focus on the topic of "SEO best practices." By repeating the theme of SEO across different pieces of content, the company can establish itself as an expert in that area and improve its search rankings for related keywords.

Real-World Example: HubSpot's Inbound Marketing Content

HubSpot, a leader in inbound marketing, uses repetition effectively in its content marketing strategy. HubSpot's blog, eBooks, webinars, and online courses consistently focus on key topics like inbound marketing, lead generation, and CRM software. By repeatedly publishing content on these topics, HubSpot has established itself as a go-to resource for marketers and sales professionals.

The repetition of key messages across different formats helps HubSpot build authority, attract organic traffic, and convert leads into paying customers.

Key Takeaway:

Repetition in content marketing helps reinforce key messages and build trust over time. Repurposing content and maintaining consistency across platforms ensures that your audience encounters your message multiple times, increasing the chances of conversion.

5: Balancing Repetition with Freshness

Avoiding Over-Repetition and Ad Fatigue

While repetition is a powerful tool, there's a fine line between reinforcing your message and over-repeating it to the point where it becomes stale or annoying. **Ad fatigue** occurs when consumers are exposed to the same ad or message too many times, leading to diminishing returns and even negative associations with the brand.

Signs of ad fatigue include:

- Decreasing engagement rates (clicks, likes, shares).
- Increasing cost-per-click (CPC) in paid campaigns.
- Negative comments or feedback from consumers.

To avoid over-repetition, it's important to balance consistency with freshness. This means maintaining your core message while finding new and creative ways to present it.

Strategies to Keep Repetition Fresh

1. **Vary the Format**: Even if you're repeating the same message, you can keep it fresh by varying the format. For example, if you've been running static banner ads, try switching to video ads. If your blog content has been text-heavy, experiment with infographics or interactive content.
2. **Use Different Storytelling Angles**: Another way to keep repetition fresh is by using different storytelling angles to convey the same message. For example, a fitness brand that emphasizes the benefits of regular exercise could create one campaign focused on mental health benefits and another focused on physical health benefits.
3. **Rotate Creatives**: In paid advertising, rotating creatives (e.g., changing visuals, headlines, or copy) helps prevent ad fatigue while still maintaining the

same underlying message. For example, a brand might rotate between three or four different versions of a Facebook ad, each with a slightly different image or copy, to keep the audience engaged.

4. **Segment Your Audience**: By segmenting your audience, you can tailor your message to different groups without over-repeating the same content. For example, an eCommerce brand could create one campaign for returning customers and another for first-time visitors, both reinforcing the brand's core message but with different angles.
5. **Update and Refresh Older Content**: If you've been running the same campaign for an extended period, consider refreshing it with updated visuals, new statistics, or current events. This allows you to continue reinforcing your message without it feeling dated.

Real-World Example: Starbucks Holiday Campaigns

Starbucks is known for its seasonal campaigns, particularly during the holiday season. Each year, the brand repeats its core holiday messaging—warmth, tradition, and togetherness—while introducing new drinks, festive cups, and fresh visuals. This repetition helps create a sense of familiarity and excitement around the Starbucks brand during the holidays, while the annual updates keep the campaign feeling fresh and engaging.

Measuring the Impact of Repetition

To ensure that your repetition strategy is effective and not leading to fatigue, it's important to continuously monitor key performance indicators (KPIs), such as:

- **Engagement rates**: Are people interacting with your ads or content at the same rate, or are they losing interest?
- **Conversion rates**: Are your repeated messages leading to conversions, or is there a decline in performance over time?
- **Audience feedback**: What are consumers saying about your brand? Are they leaving positive comments, or are there signs of frustration?

By regularly reviewing these metrics, you can adjust your strategy to maintain the right balance between repetition and freshness.

Key Takeaway:

Repetition must be balanced with creativity to avoid fatigue. Use varied formats, storytelling angles, and audience segmentation to keep your message fresh while maintaining consistency.

Conclusion: The Long-Term Benefits of Repetition

Repetition is one of the most powerful tools in marketing, helping brands build familiarity, trust, and loyalty over time. From consistent branding and messaging to repeated exposure through advertising and content marketing, repetition creates a strong foundation for long-term success.

The Cumulative Effect of Repetition

The cumulative effect of repetition cannot be overstated. While a single exposure to a message or brand may not lead to immediate action, repeated exposure increases the likelihood that consumers will remember and trust the brand when they are ready to make a purchase. Over time, these repeated touchpoints compound, leading to stronger brand equity and higher conversion rates.

Key Lessons on Repetition in Marketing

1. **Consistency is key**: Repeating your core message across all channels creates a cohesive and recognizable brand identity.
2. **Repetition builds trust**: The more consumers see your message, the more familiar and trustworthy your brand becomes.
3. **Repetition works across channels**: Effective repetition occurs not only in a single channel but across multiple platforms, from social media to email marketing to paid ads.
4. **Balance is crucial**: While repetition is important, it must be balanced with freshness and creativity to avoid audience fatigue.

Final Thought

Repetition is not about bombarding your audience with the same message until they give in; it's about creating a steady drumbeat that reinforces your brand's value over time. When used effectively, repetition can transform fleeting interactions into lasting relationships and casual visitors into loyal customers.

By mastering the art of repetition, you can create marketing campaigns that resonate deeply with your audience and build long-term brand success.

Chapter 13

HOW TO SCALE AN IRRESISTIBLE OFFER

Scaling an irresistible offer is the ultimate goal of any business seeking to grow its revenue, customer base, and brand presence. While creating a compelling offer that resonates with your target audience is critical, scaling that offer successfully requires a strategic approach. Scaling involves optimizing every aspect of your offer—from marketing and distribution to customer acquisition and retention—so that it can reach more people, convert better, and continue delivering value at a larger scale.

In this chapter, we'll explore the core strategies for scaling an irresistible offer, including refining your value proposition, leveraging automation and systems, optimizing marketing and sales funnels, expanding into new channels, and retaining customers for the long term. By the end, you will have a clear understanding of how to take an offer that works on a small scale and transform it into a revenue-generating engine that can fuel sustainable growth.

1: Laying the Foundation for Scale

Understanding Your Offer's Core Value

Before you begin scaling your offer, you need to have a clear understanding of its core value. Your offer is more than just a product or service—it's the promise you make to your customers and the unique value you deliver that sets you apart from competitors. To successfully scale your offer, you need to ensure that this value proposition remains compelling, even as you grow.

Start by asking the following questions:

- **What problem does your offer solve?** Ensure that the problem your offer addresses is relevant to a broad audience. If your offer solves a niche problem, consider how you can adapt it to appeal to a wider market while maintaining its uniqueness.
- **What is the primary benefit of your offer?** Focus on the key benefits that your target audience cares about the most. These benefits should remain consistent, even as you scale.
- **Why should customers choose your offer over competitors?** Your unique selling proposition (USP) is critical for standing out in a crowded marketplace. Scaling your offer requires you to maintain or even enhance this competitive edge.

Ensuring Scalability from the Start

One of the biggest challenges in scaling an offer is ensuring that the infrastructure, resources, and systems are in place to handle increased demand. To avoid growing pains and bottlenecks, you need to design your offer with scalability in mind from the very beginning. Here's how to do it:

1. **Automate Where Possible**: Whether it's customer onboarding, fulfillment, or marketing processes, automation is key to handling increased volume without adding significant overhead. Tools like email marketing automation, customer relationship management (CRM) systems, and automated billing can save time and prevent errors as you scale.
2. **Develop Efficient Systems**: Create clear, repeatable processes for every aspect of your business. This includes product development, customer service, and fulfillment. Documenting these systems allows you to scale efficiently by reducing the need for constant oversight and minimizing human error.
3. **Build a Scalable Team**: Ensure that your team can grow with your offer. This may involve hiring key roles early on, such as a dedicated marketing manager or customer support staff, or outsourcing tasks to freelancers or agencies that can handle increased workloads.
4. **Test for Scalability**: Before expanding your offer, test its scalability by gradually increasing traffic or demand. For example, you could run a limited-time promotion to gauge how well your systems handle a spike in orders. This testing phase allows you to identify any potential weaknesses in your processes.

Key Takeaway:

The foundation of scaling an irresistible offer lies in having a deep understanding of your core value and building efficient, scalable systems from the start. Automating processes, developing repeatable systems, and testing for scalability will prepare your offer to handle increased demand as you grow.

2: Optimizing Your Sales Funnel for Scale

The Importance of a Scalable Sales Funnel

Your sales funnel is the engine that drives leads through the customer journey, from initial awareness to final conversion. As you scale, it's essential to optimize your funnel to handle more traffic, convert more leads, and maximize revenue without losing efficiency. A well-optimized sales funnel can scale seamlessly, while a poorly structured funnel can bottleneck your growth efforts.

Mapping Out Your Sales Funnel

The first step in scaling your sales funnel is to map out the key stages, which typically include:

1. **Awareness**: The top of the funnel, where prospects become aware of your offer. This is usually driven by marketing efforts such as paid ads, content marketing, and social media.
2. **Interest**: In the middle of the funnel, prospects express interest in your offer and begin to evaluate whether it's a good fit for them. This stage is

influenced by lead magnets, email marketing, and webinars.

3. **Decision**: At the bottom of the funnel, prospects are ready to make a decision and convert into paying customers. Conversion tactics here include sales pages, retargeting ads, and personalized offers.
4. **Action**: Finally, this is the stage where customers complete their purchase or sign up for your offer. Ensuring a seamless checkout process or sign-up experience is critical to minimizing friction and reducing drop-offs.

Key Metrics to Monitor in a Scalable Funnel

To optimize your sales funnel for scale, you need to closely monitor several key performance metrics (KPIs). These metrics provide insight into how effectively your funnel is performing and where improvements are needed:

- **Conversion Rate**: The percentage of prospects who move from one stage of the funnel to the next. For example, how many visitors to your website sign up for a lead magnet, or how many email subscribers ultimately purchase your offer?
- **Cost Per Acquisition (CPA)**: The cost of acquiring a new customer. As you scale, you'll want to ensure that your CPA remains sustainable and that you aren't spending more to acquire customers than the revenue they generate.
- **Lifetime Value (LTV)**: The total revenue a customer generates over their relationship with your business. Optimizing LTV is crucial for

scaling, as it allows you to invest more in customer acquisition without sacrificing profitability.

- **Churn Rate**: The rate at which customers stop using your product or service. Reducing churn becomes increasingly important as you scale, especially if you offer a subscription-based product.

Scaling Lead Generation

Scaling your offer requires scaling your lead generation efforts. If you rely on a single source of leads, you risk stalling your growth. Instead, you should diversify your lead generation channels to reach a broader audience. Some strategies for scaling lead generation include:

- **Paid Advertising**: Increase your ad spend across platforms like Google Ads, Facebook Ads, and Instagram to drive more traffic to your offer. Use retargeting to re-engage visitors who didn't convert on their first visit.
- **Content Marketing**: Publish more content to attract organic traffic from search engines. This might involve creating blog posts, video content, podcasts, or social media content that aligns with your audience's interests.
- **Webinars and Live Events**: Host webinars or live events that provide value to your audience and promote your offer at the end. This is an effective way to build trust and generate leads at scale.
- **Referral Programs**: Encourage your existing customers to refer others to your offer. By incentivizing referrals with discounts or bonuses, you can tap into a new pool of potential customers.

Automating the Funnel

To scale effectively, your sales funnel must be as automated as possible. Manual processes will quickly become unsustainable as your traffic and lead volume grow. Here are some key areas to automate:

- **Email Sequences**: Use automated email sequences to nurture leads and move them through the funnel. For example, set up a welcome series for new subscribers and a follow-up sequence for webinar attendees.
- **Lead Scoring**: Implement lead scoring to automatically prioritize leads based on their engagement and behavior. For example, you might assign higher scores to leads who open emails, click links, or visit specific pages on your website.
- **CRM Integration**: Use a CRM system to track and manage leads throughout the customer journey. Automate reminders for follow-ups, and use workflows to trigger specific actions based on lead behavior.
- **Cart Abandonment Emails**: For eCommerce or subscription-based offers, automate cart abandonment emails to remind potential customers to complete their purchase.

Optimizing the Bottom of the Funnel for Conversions

The bottom of the funnel (BoFu) is where the final conversion happens. Optimizing this stage for scalability is critical because even small improvements here can lead to significant gains in revenue. Strategies for optimizing BoFu conversions include:

- **A/B Testing**: Continuously test different versions of your sales pages, CTAs, and pricing models to identify the elements that convert the best.
- **Simplify Checkout**: Ensure that the checkout or sign-up process is as simple and frictionless as possible. Remove unnecessary steps, offer guest checkout, and use trusted payment methods.
- **Offer Social Proof**: Display testimonials, reviews, and case studies on your sales pages to build trust and reduce objections. Customers are more likely to convert when they see that others have had positive experiences with your offer.

Key Takeaway:

To scale your offer, you need a sales funnel that can handle increased traffic, convert leads efficiently, and maximize revenue. By optimizing each stage of the funnel, diversifying your lead generation channels, and automating key processes, you can build a scalable funnel that drives sustained growth.

3: Expanding into New Channels

Why Expanding Channels is Critical for Scaling

Relying on a single marketing channel limits the growth potential of your offer. As you scale, it's essential to expand into new channels to reach a wider audience, mitigate risks, and drive more traffic to your funnel. By diversifying your channels, you reduce the risk of being overly reliant on one platform and increase your chances of finding new customers.

Identifying High-Potential Channels

To scale effectively, it's important to identify which channels have the highest potential for driving growth. Here's how to evaluate new channels:

- **Audience Fit**: Does your target audience actively use the channel? For example, if your offer is aimed at professionals, LinkedIn might be a more effective platform than Instagram.
- **Cost Per Acquisition (CPA)**: What is the average CPA for the channel? You want to focus on channels that offer a balance of reach and cost-effectiveness.
- **Scalability**: Is the channel scalable? Some channels, like organic search, take time to build but offer long-term scalability, while others, like paid ads, can deliver immediate traffic but may become cost-prohibitive as you scale.
- **Competitive Landscape**: How competitive is the channel? If your industry is highly competitive on a particular platform, it may be more expensive or difficult to break through the noise.

Paid Advertising Channels

Paid advertising is one of the fastest ways to scale an offer, as it allows you to reach a large audience quickly. Here are some key paid channels to consider:

1. **Google Ads**: Google Ads allows you to target users who are actively searching for solutions related to your offer. This is a high-intent audience, making it one of the most effective paid channels for driving conversions. Use both search and display ads to reach users across the web.
2. **Facebook and Instagram Ads**: These platforms offer highly targeted advertising options, allowing you to reach specific demographics based on interests, behaviors, and online activity. Facebook and Instagram ads are particularly effective for driving brand awareness and lead generation.
3. **LinkedIn Ads**: LinkedIn is ideal for B2B offers, as it allows you to target professionals based on their job title, industry, and company size. This platform is particularly useful for scaling high-ticket offers or services aimed at corporate clients.
4. **YouTube Ads**: Video advertising on YouTube allows you to reach a massive audience and demonstrate the value of your offer in a highly engaging format. Use YouTube ads to drive traffic to your sales funnel or promote your brand through educational content.

Organic and Content-Based Channels

While paid advertising can deliver quick results, organic and content-based channels offer long-term scalability and help build credibility. Here are some content-driven channels to explore:

1. **Search Engine Optimization (SEO)**: Ranking for high-intent keywords in search engines like Google

can generate a steady stream of organic traffic over time. Invest in creating high-quality content, such as blog posts, guides, and videos, that target keywords your audience is searching for.

2. **Content Marketing**: Publishing regular content on your blog, YouTube channel, or podcast helps you build authority and attract an audience over time. Use your content to educate, inform, and entertain your audience while subtly promoting your offer.
3. **Social Media**: Social media platforms like Instagram, Twitter, and TikTok offer opportunities to reach a broad audience through organic posts, hashtags, and influencer collaborations. Consistently posting engaging content can help you grow your following and drive traffic to your sales funnel.
4. **Affiliate Marketing**: Partnering with affiliates or influencers who promote your offer in exchange for a commission can help you scale without upfront advertising costs. Affiliates provide access to new audiences and can help drive traffic and conversions at scale.

Leveraging Omnichannel Strategies

An omnichannel strategy involves using multiple channels to create a seamless and integrated experience for your customers. For example, a customer might first encounter your offer through a Facebook ad, read a blog post on your website, receive an email with a special promotion, and then see a retargeting ad on Google. Each touchpoint reinforces the previous one, increasing the likelihood of conversion.

Here's how to create an effective omnichannel strategy:

- **Consistent Messaging**: Ensure that your messaging is consistent across all channels. Whether a customer encounters your brand on social media, in an email, or on your website, they should receive the same core message and value proposition.
- **Unified Customer Experience**: Create a seamless experience by integrating your channels. For example, if a customer abandons their cart on your website, they should receive an email reminder and see retargeting ads that encourage them to complete the purchase.
- **Data Integration**: Use data from each channel to inform your strategy. For example, if a customer clicks on a Facebook ad but doesn't convert, use retargeting ads on Google to follow up with a tailored offer.

Key Takeaway:

Expanding into new channels is essential for scaling your offer and reaching a wider audience. Paid advertising delivers quick results, while organic and content-driven channels provide long-term growth opportunities. An omnichannel strategy ensures that your message is reinforced across multiple touchpoints, driving conversions at scale.

4: Leveraging Automation to Scale Efficiently

Why Automation is Key to Scaling

As your offer grows, managing leads, customers, and processes manually becomes increasingly difficult. Automation allows you to scale efficiently by streamlining repetitive tasks, improving accuracy, and freeing up your team to focus on higher-value activities. With automation, you can manage a growing customer base, optimize your marketing efforts, and improve the customer experience without exponentially increasing costs or time spent.

Automating Lead Generation and Nurturing

Automating lead generation and nurturing is one of the most effective ways to scale your marketing efforts. By using marketing automation tools, you can capture leads, follow up with personalized messages, and move prospects through your sales funnel without requiring manual intervention.

1. **Lead Capture Forms**: Use lead capture forms on your website, landing pages, and social media to automatically collect contact information from interested prospects. These forms should be integrated with your CRM or email marketing platform to ensure leads are captured and segmented properly.
2. **Email Nurturing Campaigns**: Set up automated email sequences to nurture leads over time. For example, when a new subscriber signs up for your email list, they can be automatically enrolled in a

welcome series that educates them about your brand and gradually introduces your offer.

3. **Segmentation and Personalization**: Use automation tools to segment your leads based on behavior (e.g., pages visited, emails opened) and demographics (e.g., location, industry). By sending personalized emails or offers, you can increase engagement and conversion rates.
4. **Retargeting Campaigns**: Automate retargeting ads to follow up with leads who have shown interest in your offer but haven't converted. For example, if a visitor adds an item to their cart but doesn't complete the purchase, they can automatically see retargeting ads on Facebook or Google reminding them to return and buy.

Scaling Customer Support with Automation

As your customer base grows, providing timely and efficient support becomes more challenging. Automation can help scale your customer support efforts by handling common queries, providing self-service options, and routing complex issues to the appropriate team members.

1. **Chatbots**: Implement chatbots on your website to handle common customer questions, such as product availability, shipping times, or troubleshooting. Chatbots provide instant responses and can operate 24/7, ensuring that customers receive support even outside of business hours.
2. **Help Centers and FAQs**: Create a robust help center or FAQ section where customers can

find answers to their questions without needing to contact support. This reduces the volume of support tickets and allows your team to focus on more complex issues.

3. **Automated Ticket Routing**: Use automation tools to route customer support tickets to the appropriate team members based on the nature of the inquiry. For example, technical issues can be automatically sent to the IT team, while billing questions are routed to the finance team.
4. **Customer Feedback Surveys**: Automate customer satisfaction surveys to gather feedback after interactions with support. This helps you identify areas for improvement and ensures that customers feel heard.

Automating Sales Processes

Automation can also streamline your sales processes, allowing your sales team to focus on high-value activities like closing deals. Here are some ways to automate sales processes:

1. **Lead Scoring**: Automatically assign scores to leads based on their engagement with your content, such as email opens, website visits, or demo requests. This helps your sales team prioritize leads that are most likely to convert.
2. **CRM Automation**: Use a CRM system to automate tasks like follow-up reminders, appointment scheduling, and pipeline management. This ensures that leads don't fall through the cracks and allows your sales team to manage a larger volume of prospects.

3. **Automated Proposals and Contracts**: Use automation tools to generate and send proposals, quotes, and contracts. This speeds up the sales process and ensures consistency across all communications.

Key Takeaway:

Automation is essential for scaling your offer efficiently. By automating lead generation, nurturing, customer support, and sales processes, you can handle increased demand without sacrificing quality or speed. Automation frees up your team to focus on high-value activities while ensuring a seamless customer experience.

5: Scaling Customer Acquisition and Retention

Scaling Customer Acquisition

Acquiring new customers is one of the most challenging aspects of scaling an offer. As you grow, the cost of acquiring customers (CAC) can increase, and it becomes more difficult to find new audiences. To scale customer acquisition effectively, you need a combination of paid and organic strategies, as well as optimization tactics that ensure you're getting the most value from every dollar spent.

1. Paid Acquisition Strategies

Scaling customer acquisition through paid channels requires careful management of your ad spend, targeting, and messaging. Here's how to scale paid acquisition:

- **Increase Ad Spend Strategically**: Start by increasing your ad spend on channels that have proven to deliver the best ROI. This could be Google Ads, Facebook Ads, or LinkedIn Ads. However, be mindful of diminishing returns—there is often a point where increased spend no longer results in proportional returns. Monitor your CPA and adjust accordingly.
- **Use Lookalike Audiences**: Platforms like Facebook allow you to create lookalike audiences based on your existing customers. These audiences share similar characteristics with your best customers, making them more likely to convert. Scaling with lookalike audiences is an effective way to reach new customers without starting from scratch.
- **Leverage Retargeting**: As your traffic increases, retargeting becomes an even more powerful tool for scaling acquisition. Set up retargeting campaigns to show ads to visitors who didn't convert the first time around. This ensures that you're maximizing the value of every website visit.
- **Test New Ad Platforms**: Once you've maximized your primary ad channels, consider testing new platforms to reach different audiences. For example, TikTok ads may be effective for younger demographics, while Pinterest ads can work well for visual-driven brands like home decor or fashion.

2. Organic Acquisition Strategies

While paid acquisition can deliver quick wins, organic strategies are critical for long-term scaling because they provide a steady stream of traffic without ongoing ad costs. Here are some ways to scale organic acquisition:

- **SEO and Content Marketing**: Invest in SEO and content marketing to drive organic traffic over time. This might involve creating high-quality blog posts, videos, or infographics that rank for relevant search terms. Over time, these efforts compound and result in consistent traffic growth.
- **Social Media Growth**: Building a strong presence on social media platforms can help you acquire customers organically. Focus on growing your following by posting engaging content, interacting with your audience, and leveraging user-generated content (UGC). Social media can also amplify word-of-mouth marketing, which is invaluable for scaling.
- **Partnerships and Collaborations**: Partner with other brands, influencers, or content creators in your industry to reach new audiences. For example, co-hosting a webinar or creating a joint content piece can introduce your offer to a larger audience.

Scaling Customer Retention

While acquiring new customers is essential for growth, scaling retention is equally important. Retaining customers allows you to increase their lifetime value (LTV), reduce churn, and create a loyal customer base that supports your long-term success.

1. Provide a Seamless Onboarding Experience

Customer retention starts with a positive onboarding experience. The smoother the onboarding process, the more likely customers are to stay and engage with your offer. Here's how to scale your onboarding process:

- **Automate Onboarding**: Use automated emails, tutorials, or videos to guide new customers through the onboarding process. These resources should help customers get the most value out of your offer quickly and easily.
- **Personalize the Experience**: Use customer data to personalize the onboarding experience. For example, if a customer signs up for your software, tailor the onboarding process based on their specific use case or industry.

2. Implement a Loyalty Program

Loyalty programs are a proven way to increase customer retention and encourage repeat purchases. By rewarding customers for their continued engagement, you create a sense of appreciation and incentivize future purchases. Here's how to implement a scalable loyalty program:

- **Point-Based Systems**: Offer customers points for every purchase or action they take (e.g., leaving a review, referring a friend). These points can be redeemed for discounts, free products, or exclusive rewards.
- **Tiered Programs**: Create tiered loyalty programs that offer increasing benefits as customers spend more or engage more frequently. For example, you might have Bronze, Silver, and Gold tiers, with each tier offering better perks like free shipping, early access to new products, or VIP customer support.

3. Reduce Churn with Proactive Support

Proactively addressing customer issues can help reduce churn and keep customers engaged with your offer. Here's how to scale proactive support:

- **Regular Check-Ins**: Automate check-in emails that ask customers how they're enjoying the product or if they need any help. This shows that you care about their experience and provides an opportunity to resolve any issues before they become reasons to cancel.
- **Surveys and Feedback**: Use surveys to gather feedback on how your offer can be improved. By acting on this feedback, you show customers that you're listening and making changes to enhance their experience.

Measuring Retention Success

To measure the success of your retention efforts, track the following metrics:

- **Churn Rate**: The percentage of customers who cancel or stop using your offer over a specific period. Reducing churn is key to scaling your offer sustainably.
- **Customer Lifetime Value (LTV)**: The total revenue generated by a customer over their relationship with your business. Increasing LTV allows you to invest more in customer acquisition while maintaining profitability.

- **Repeat Purchase Rate**: The percentage of customers who make more than one purchase. A higher repeat purchase rate indicates strong customer loyalty and satisfaction.

Key Takeaway:

Scaling customer acquisition and retention is critical for sustainable growth. By leveraging paid and organic acquisition strategies, investing in retention through onboarding, loyalty programs, and proactive support, you can create a scalable system that drives long-term success.

Conclusion: Building a Scalable Offer for Long-Term Success

Scaling an irresistible offer is both an art and a science. While creating a compelling offer that resonates with your audience is the first step, successfully scaling that offer requires careful planning, optimization, and execution across all areas of your business. From optimizing your sales funnel and expanding into new channels to leveraging automation and scaling both customer acquisition and retention, each element plays a crucial role in the process.

The Keys to Scaling Success

1. **Build a Strong Foundation**: Ensure that your offer is scalable from the start by automating processes, building efficient systems, and understanding your core value proposition.
2. **Optimize Your Sales Funnel**: Create a sales funnel that is optimized for scalability by automating

key processes, improving conversion rates, and diversifying your lead generation channels.

3. **Expand into New Channels**: Diversify your marketing efforts by expanding into new paid and organic channels. Use an omnichannel strategy to create a seamless customer experience across all touchpoints.
4. **Leverage Automation**: Automate lead generation, customer support, and sales processes to handle increased demand efficiently and free up your team for higher-value tasks.
5. **Scale Customer Acquisition and Retention**: Focus on scaling both customer acquisition and retention to maximize revenue and minimize churn. Invest in paid advertising, content marketing, and loyalty programs to drive long-term success.

Final Thought

Scaling an offer is an ongoing process that requires continuous optimization and adaptation. As your offer grows, you'll need to regularly assess your systems, strategies, and customer feedback to ensure that you're meeting the evolving needs of your audience. By staying focused on delivering value at scale, you can transform an irresistible offer into a sustainable growth engine that drives your business forward for years to come.

Chapter 14

DOMINATING YOUR MARKET WITH IRRESISTIBLE OFFERS

In the highly competitive landscape of digital marketing, creating an irresistible offer is one of the most powerful strategies for standing out from the crowd and dominating your market. While many businesses rely on incremental improvements in their products or services, the ability to craft an offer so compelling that it's impossible for customers to refuse is a game-changer. An irresistible offer can catapult a business ahead of competitors, drive massive sales, and create a loyal customer base that keeps coming back.

In this chapter, we'll explore how to create, refine, and leverage irresistible offers to dominate your market. We'll delve into the psychology behind customer decision-making, how to differentiate your offer from competitors, and the strategies you need to position your business as the top choice in your industry.

1: Understanding What Makes an Offer Irresistible

The Elements of an Irresistible Offer

At its core, an irresistible offer is one that aligns perfectly with your target audience's needs, desires, and pain points. It's designed to eliminate hesitation, create a sense of urgency, and make it easy for the customer to say "yes." To dominate your market with such an offer, you need to master the key elements that make it truly compelling:

1. **Clear Value Proposition**: Your offer must clearly communicate the value it delivers to the customer. The benefits of your product or service should be front and center, making it obvious why the customer should choose you over competitors.
2. **Perceived Value**: The perceived value of your offer needs to exceed its price. This means that your audience should feel like they're getting much more than they're paying for. Offering bonuses, guarantees, or exclusive benefits can enhance the perceived value.
3. **Risk Reversal**: People are naturally hesitant to part with their money, especially if there's uncertainty about the outcome. By offering risk reversal techniques—such as money-back guarantees, free trials, or "pay only if satisfied" models—you can eliminate the customer's fear of making the wrong decision.
4. **Scarcity and Urgency**: One of the most powerful drivers of customer action is the fear of missing out

(FOMO). Limited-time offers, exclusive bonuses for early adopters, or restricting the number of available units can create a sense of urgency, prompting customers to act immediately.

5. **Social Proof**: Potential customers are more likely to trust an offer if they see that others have already had positive experiences. Testimonials, case studies, reviews, and endorsements help to build credibility and trust, making your offer more attractive.

The Psychology of Irresistible Offers

To create an offer that dominates your market, you need to understand the psychology behind customer behavior. Some key psychological principles include:

- **Loss Aversion**: People are more motivated by the fear of losing something than by the potential of gaining something. A limited-time discount or bonus that will disappear if they don't act creates a powerful incentive to buy.
- **Reciprocity**: When you give something of value to your audience (such as free content, discounts, or bonuses), they feel a psychological obligation to return the favor by making a purchase.
- **Anchoring**: Consumers tend to rely heavily on the first piece of information they encounter when making decisions. This is why pricing comparisons work so well. By offering a premium option alongside your standard offer, you can make the standard offer seem like an incredible deal by comparison.

Key Takeaway:

To dominate your market with an irresistible offer, focus on maximizing perceived value, minimizing risk, and leveraging psychological triggers like loss aversion and reciprocity. The clearer and more compelling your offer is, the easier it will be for your target audience to choose you over competitors.

2: Differentiating Your Offer from Competitors

Standing Out in a Crowded Market

In most industries, competition is fierce. Many businesses offer similar products or services, often at comparable price points. To dominate your market, your offer must stand out from the rest. Here are some ways to differentiate your offer:

1. **Unique Selling Proposition (USP)**: Your USP is what sets you apart from competitors. It's the unique benefit or feature that only you can offer, and it should be central to your marketing message. Whether it's faster delivery, higher quality, or a unique customer experience, your USP needs to be compelling enough to make customers choose you.
2. **Bonus Add-Ons**: One of the easiest ways to differentiate your offer is by adding bonuses that competitors don't include. For example, if you sell an online course, you could offer free coaching sessions, templates, or an exclusive community as a bonus. These extras enhance the perceived value and make your offer more attractive than others in the market.

3. **Better Customer Experience**: Sometimes, the offer itself may be similar to what your competitors are providing, but you can differentiate yourself through superior customer service and support. Offering personalized service, fast response times, and a hassle-free return policy can create a competitive edge.
4. **Brand Positioning**: Your brand's position in the market—whether as a premium provider, budget-friendly option, or specialized expert—can also help differentiate your offer. For example, Apple positions its products as premium, focusing on quality, innovation, and design, while other brands compete on price.

Real-World Example: Dollar Shave Club vs. Gillette

Dollar Shave Club famously disrupted the razor market by offering a subscription service that provided razors at a much lower price than traditional competitors like Gillette. While Gillette dominated the market with high-quality, premium-priced razors, Dollar Shave Club focused on affordability and convenience.

In addition to the low price point, Dollar Shave Club differentiated itself with humorous, relatable marketing that resonated with younger, cost-conscious consumers. They also offered a "cancel anytime" policy, which reduced the risk for new customers. This combination of a unique offer, strong branding, and risk reversal helped Dollar Shave Club dominate its market.

Finding Your Niche

Another way to differentiate your offer is by targeting a specific niche within your broader market. Instead of trying to appeal to everyone, focus on a smaller, highly targeted group of customers with specific needs or interests. By becoming the go-to provider for this niche, you can dominate that segment of the market and build a loyal customer base.

Steps to Identify and Dominate a Niche:

- **Research Your Market**: Identify underserved groups or pain points within your broader market. Look for gaps that competitors aren't addressing.
- **Tailor Your Offer**: Create an offer that is highly relevant to your chosen niche. This could mean adding features, bonuses, or services that cater specifically to their needs.
- **Speak Their Language**: Use messaging and branding that resonates with your niche audience. Show them that you understand their unique challenges and can provide the best solution.

Key Takeaway:

To differentiate your offer and dominate your market, focus on your unique selling proposition, offer valuable bonuses, and provide an exceptional customer experience. Targeting a specific niche within your market can also give you a competitive edge by addressing the unique needs of a focused audience.

3: Creating a Dominating Offer Framework

Step 1: Identifying Your Core Offer

The first step in building an offer that dominates your market is identifying your core offer. This is the primary product or service that provides the most value to your customers and serves as the foundation for all other elements of your marketing strategy. Your core offer should be:

- **Aligned with Customer Needs**: Ensure that your offer addresses a significant pain point or desire that your audience has. The more relevant and valuable your solution is, the more likely it will resonate with customers.
- **Simple and Clear**: Don't overcomplicate your core offer with too many options or confusing terms. The more straightforward and easy to understand your offer is, the more likely customers will take action.
- **Positioned for Impact**: Your core offer should be positioned as a solution that delivers immediate and meaningful results. Highlight the benefits your customers will experience as soon as they purchase or sign up.

Step 2: Adding Bonuses and Enhancements

To create an irresistible offer that dominates your market, consider layering additional bonuses and enhancements on top of your core offer. Bonuses increase the perceived value of your offer without significantly increasing your costs. Here are some examples:

- **Digital Bonuses**: If you sell a physical product, consider offering digital bonuses like an eBook, exclusive video content, or downloadable guides. These bonuses cost little to deliver but can significantly increase the perceived value of your offer.
- **Membership or Community Access**: Many successful businesses create exclusive communities around their offers. For example, when customers purchase your product or service, they could gain access to a private Facebook group, members-only webinars, or a VIP customer support line.
- **Free Upgrades or Add-Ons**: Offering free upgrades or complementary products can be a powerful incentive for customers to choose your offer. For example, a software company might offer additional premium features for free if customers sign up within a limited time.

Step 3: Implementing Risk Reversal

To further enhance the attractiveness of your offer, implement **risk reversal** techniques. Risk reversal shifts the perceived risk from the customer to the seller, making it easier for potential buyers to say "yes."

Some common forms of risk reversal include:

- **Money-Back Guarantee**: Offering a no-questions-asked money-back guarantee reduces the perceived risk of trying your product or service. This is particularly effective for high-ticket offers, where the customer may be hesitant to commit without some assurance.

- **Free Trials**: For digital products or services, offering a free trial allows customers to experience the benefits of your offer without financial commitment. This can be especially effective in industries like software, where customers may need time to evaluate the product.
- **"Pay If You're Satisfied"**: This model allows customers to use your product or service and only pay if they are satisfied with the results. While not suitable for every business, this approach can be a powerful way to overcome objections and gain trust.

Step 4: Creating Urgency and Scarcity

To dominate your market, your offer needs to compel customers to take action now, rather than delaying their decision. Creating a sense of urgency and scarcity is one of the most effective ways to do this. Some strategies include:

- **Limited-Time Discounts**: Offer a discount that expires within a certain time frame, such as 24 hours or a week. This encourages customers to act quickly to avoid missing out on savings.
- **Exclusive Access**: Create exclusivity by offering limited access to your product or service. For example, you could offer your product to the first 100 buyers or restrict access to a new feature for a limited group of customers.

- **Limited Availability**: Scarcity drives action by making customers feel that if they don't act now, they might miss out. For example, "only 10 spots left" or "limited stock available" are powerful motivators that push customers to buy before it's too late.

Step 5: Using Social Proof to Build Trust

Social proof is a critical component of any market-dominating offer. People are more likely to trust your offer if they see that others have already had positive experiences. Here are some ways to use social proof effectively:

- **Testimonials and Reviews**: Display customer testimonials or reviews prominently on your website, sales pages, and marketing materials. Include specific results or benefits that customers experienced after using your offer.
- **Case Studies**: Share detailed case studies that show how your product or service helped customers achieve their goals. Case studies provide credibility and demonstrate the real-world value of your offer.
- **Influencer Endorsements**: Partner with influencers or industry experts who can endorse your offer. This adds an additional layer of trust and credibility, especially for audiences that follow those influencers.

Key Takeaway:

By following this framework, you can create a powerful offer that not only captures attention but compels customers to take immediate action. Identifying your core offer, enhancing it with bonuses, implementing risk reversal, creating urgency, and leveraging social proof will position you as the go-to choice in your market.

4: Scaling Your Offer for Market Domination

Building a Sales Funnel for Maximum Reach

Scaling an irresistible offer requires an efficient sales funnel that guides leads from awareness to conversion. To dominate your market, your funnel needs to be optimized for both lead generation and sales conversion. Here's how to create a scalable funnel:

1. **Attracting Traffic**: Start by driving traffic to your offer through a mix of paid advertising, organic search, social media, and content marketing. The more targeted your traffic sources, the higher your conversion rates will be.
2. **Lead Magnets**: Offer a valuable lead magnet, such as a free eBook, webinar, or checklist, in exchange for the visitor's email address. This allows you to build a relationship with potential customers over time.
3. **Email Nurturing**: Use automated email sequences to nurture leads and provide additional value. Gradually introduce your offer, highlighting the benefits, addressing common objections, and including strong calls to action.
4. **Sales Pages**: Your sales page should be designed to convert leads into customers. Use persuasive copy, strong visuals, and compelling testimonials to build trust and guide visitors toward purchasing.

- **Follow-Up Sequences**: For visitors who don't convert immediately, use follow-up emails, retargeting ads, and special offers to re-engage them and drive conversions. Often, it takes several touchpoints before a customer is ready to buy.

Expanding Your Offer Across Multiple Channels

To dominate your market, you need to reach your audience across multiple channels. This ensures that your offer is seen by a broad audience and allows you to build a strong presence in the market. Some channels to consider include:

1. **Paid Advertising**: Use platforms like Google Ads, Facebook Ads, and Instagram Ads to target specific audiences with highly personalized messaging. Paid advertising allows you to scale quickly and reach new customers at scale.
2. **Content Marketing**: Publish valuable content—such as blog posts, videos, and podcasts—that educates and informs your audience. Content marketing builds trust over time and drives organic traffic to your offer.
3. **Affiliate Marketing**: Partner with affiliates who can promote your offer to their audiences in exchange for a commission. Affiliate marketing allows you to leverage the reach and credibility of others to grow your customer base.
4. **Referral Programs**: Encourage your existing customers to refer others to your offer. By offering incentives for successful referrals, you can tap into word-of-mouth marketing and expand your reach organically.

Measuring Success and Refining Your Offer

To ensure that your offer continues to dominate the market, you need to regularly measure its performance and make improvements where necessary. Here are some key metrics to track:

1. **Conversion Rate**: Monitor the conversion rate of your sales pages, emails, and ads. If conversion rates begin to drop, test different elements of your offer, such as the price, bonuses, or sales copy.
2. **Customer Lifetime Value (LTV)**: Track the LTV of your customers to understand how much revenue each customer generates over time. Increasing LTV allows you to invest more in customer acquisition and scale faster.
3. **Churn Rate**: If you offer a subscription service, monitor your churn rate to identify potential issues that may be causing customers to leave. Reducing churn helps you retain more customers and sustain growth.
4. **Customer Feedback**: Regularly collect customer feedback through surveys, reviews, and direct communication. This feedback can provide valuable insights into how to improve your offer and better meet your customers' needs.

Continuous Optimization for Market Domination

Domination isn't a one-time achievement—it requires continuous improvement and adaptation. As market conditions, customer preferences, and competitors evolve, you need to stay ahead by refining your offer. This means:

- **Regularly Updating Bonuses**: Refresh your offer with new bonuses or enhancements to keep it attractive and competitive.
- **Adapting to Feedback**: Use customer feedback to make adjustments to your product or service, improving the overall experience.
- **Staying Innovative**: Keep an eye on trends in your industry and adapt your offer to stay relevant and ahead of the competition.

Key Takeaway:

Scaling your offer for market domination involves building an efficient sales funnel, expanding across multiple channels, and continuously measuring and optimizing your offer for sustained growth. By doing so, you'll position yourself as the leading brand in your industry.

Conclusion: The Path to Market Domination

Dominating your market with an irresistible offer is no small feat, but with the right strategy, it is entirely achievable. By understanding the psychology behind customer decision-making, differentiating your offer from competitors, creating a comprehensive offer framework, and scaling efficiently, you can build a powerful position in your industry.

Final Key Takeaways:

1. **Understand the Psychology**: Leverage psychological triggers like loss aversion, reciprocity, and anchoring to make your offer more appealing.

2. **Differentiate Your Offer**: Stand out from competitors by emphasizing your unique selling proposition, adding valuable bonuses, and offering a superior customer experience.
3. **Create an Offer Framework**: Develop a core offer, enhance it with bonuses, implement risk reversal, and create urgency to compel immediate action.
4. **Scale with a Sales Funnel**: Build an efficient sales funnel that attracts, nurtures, and converts leads. Expand across multiple channels and automate key processes for growth.
5. **Continuous Improvement**: Regularly measure the performance of your offer and make adjustments to keep it relevant, competitive, and compelling.

The Road Ahead

Market domination is not just about having the best product or service—it's about creating an offer that resonates so deeply with your audience that they choose you every time. By mastering the art of irresistible offers, you can outshine your competitors, build a loyal customer base, and achieve sustained success in your market.

Now is the time to refine your offer, scale your efforts, and position yourself as the dominant player in your industry.

Chapter 15

DESIGNING VISUALS TO ENHANCE YOUR OFFER

In the world of marketing and sales, a picture is often worth more than a thousand words. Visuals play a crucial role in shaping perceptions, guiding decisions, and enhancing the effectiveness of your offer. Whether you're promoting a product, service, or digital download, the right visual elements can significantly boost your conversion rates. Well-designed visuals attract attention, communicate your message, and build trust—all of which contribute to the overall success of your offer.

In this chapter, we will explore how to design visuals that not only complement but elevate your offer. We'll delve into the psychology of design, the various types of visuals you can use, and practical tips for creating compelling graphics that boost engagement and conversions.

1: The Importance of Visuals in Marketing

Why Visuals Matter for Your Offer

Visuals serve as the first point of contact between your offer and your audience. In today's fast-paced digital environment, users have limited attention spans, and often, their decision to engage with your offer hinges on its visual appeal. Research suggests that people process visuals up to **60,000 times faster than text**, making images a powerful tool for grabbing attention and delivering a message quickly.

Visual design isn't just about aesthetics—it's about function and impact. Effective visuals:

- **Create a strong first impression**: They help shape how potential customers perceive your brand and offer. A poorly designed visual can turn people away, while a high-quality one can make your offer stand out.
- **Increase engagement**: Posts with visuals receive **94% more views** than those without, and visual content is more likely to be shared across social media.
- **Clarify complex information**: Whether through infographics or diagrams, visuals can simplify complex data or features, making it easier for your audience to understand the value of your offer.
- **Build trust and credibility**: High-quality, professional visuals suggest that you've invested in your product or service, which makes consumers feel more confident in your offer.

The Role of Visuals in Enhancing Your Offer

To dominate the market with your offer, you must create a cohesive, visually compelling experience that resonates with your audience. Visuals are particularly effective when they:

- **Enhance the narrative**: They should tell a story that complements your offer, helping consumers see the value, transformation, or results they'll get.
- **Make your offer tangible**: If your product is digital (like an eBook or software), visuals can give it a tangible feel, making the value of the offer seem more real.
- **Highlight key features**: Use images, icons, and graphics to emphasize the most important benefits or features of your offer.
- **Break up text**: A wall of text is hard to digest. Visuals make your content easier to scan and process, which leads to higher engagement.

Key Takeaway:

Visuals are essential to the success of your offer. They grab attention, clarify your message, and build trust with your audience. To create a visually compelling offer, you must be intentional about how your images, colors, and design elements support the overall value proposition.

2: Key Design Principles for High-Impact Visuals

Design Fundamentals

Whether you're creating visuals yourself or working with a designer, it's essential to understand the core design principles that govern effective marketing visuals. These design fundamentals ensure that your visuals are not only attractive but also functional and aligned with your offer's goals.

1. Simplicity

Simplicity is one of the most important principles in design. Overly complex visuals can confuse or overwhelm your audience, detracting from your message. The goal of your visuals should be to enhance the offer, not to complicate it.

Tips for achieving simplicity:

- Stick to a limited color palette that complements your brand.
- Avoid clutter by using minimal text and whitespace.
- Focus on one main message or feature per visual element.

2. Consistency

Consistency in your visual design creates a cohesive look that helps establish your brand identity. When all elements of your offer—colors, typography, and imagery—work together, it reinforces your brand's professionalism and makes your offer more memorable.

How to ensure consistency:

- Use the same fonts, colors, and styles across all your marketing materials.
- Create a style guide to ensure consistency across channels (website, email, social media, ads).
- Align your visuals with your overall brand voice and tone.

3. Contrast

Contrast is crucial for making your visuals stand out and guiding the viewer's attention to the most important parts of your design. Without enough contrast, elements may blend together, making it harder for the viewer to understand your message.

How to use contrast effectively:

- Use contrasting colors to highlight calls to action (CTAs) or important features.
- Create contrast between text and background for readability.
- Combine large, bold fonts with smaller, subtler elements to draw focus.

4. Alignment

Proper alignment ensures that your visual elements are organized and professional-looking. It creates a sense of order and balance, making it easier for viewers to navigate your design.

Best practices for alignment:

- Use grid systems or templates to keep everything aligned.
- Ensure text, images, and buttons are aligned in a logical and visually pleasing way.
- Be consistent with spacing and margins to avoid a cluttered appearance.

5. Hierarchy

Visual hierarchy refers to the arrangement of elements in a way that guides the viewer's eye toward the most important information. By creating a hierarchy, you can ensure that viewers focus on the key aspects of your offer first.

Techniques for visual hierarchy:

- Use larger fonts for headings and smaller fonts for body text.
- Place the most important elements (like CTAs) at the top of the page or in the most prominent position.
- Use color and contrast to make certain elements stand out.

The Psychology of Color in Visual Design

Color plays a critical role in how people perceive your offer and brand. Different colors evoke different emotions and can influence how customers feel about your product or service. Understanding color psychology allows you to select colors that align with your brand's message and your audience's emotional triggers.

Color meanings:

- **Red**: Associated with excitement, urgency, and passion. Often used for CTAs to grab attention.
- **Blue**: Conveys trust, professionalism, and calm. Many financial or healthcare brands use blue to instill confidence.
- **Green**: Symbolizes growth, health, and nature. Frequently used for wellness brands or eco-friendly products.
- **Yellow**: Represents optimism and warmth but can also signify caution when used in excess.
- **Black**: Conveys luxury, elegance, and sophistication. Often used for high-end brands.

Choosing the right color palette:

- Use colors that align with your brand's values and your offer's emotional appeal.
- Limit your palette to 2-3 main colors to maintain visual harmony.
- Ensure your CTAs stand out by using contrasting colors.

Key Takeaway:

Mastering design principles such as simplicity, contrast, and visual hierarchy will help you create impactful visuals that support and enhance your offer. Additionally, understanding color psychology enables you to evoke the right emotions and guide customer behavior.

3: Types of Visuals to Use in Your Offer

Different types of visuals can enhance your offer in unique ways. The key is to select visuals that align with your offer's message and goals. In this section, we'll explore the most effective types of visuals for offers and how to use them to maximum effect.

1. Product Images

For physical products, high-quality images are essential. They allow your audience to see the product up close and understand its features, size, and quality. Investing in professional product photography can make your offer more appealing and build credibility.

Tips for effective product images:

- Use multiple angles to give a comprehensive view of the product.
- Include close-up shots of key features.
- Ensure the lighting is bright and flattering.
- Use a clean, uncluttered background to focus attention on the product.

2. Mockups for Digital Products

If your offer is digital (e.g., an eBook, software, or online course), mockups help make the offer more tangible. For example, you can show a 3D rendering of an eBook on a tablet, or a screenshot of the software in use. Mockups allow potential customers to visualize what they're purchasing.

Best practices for mockups:

- Use high-resolution images that reflect the professional quality of your product.
- Incorporate your brand's colors and style into the mockup.
- Highlight key benefits or features through overlay text or icons.

3. Infographics

Infographics are ideal for conveying complex information in an easy-to-understand visual format. They allow you to present data, statistics, or processes in a visually engaging way, making it easier for your audience to digest and retain the information.

How to create effective infographics:

- Focus on a single theme or topic to avoid overwhelming the viewer.
- Use icons, illustrations, and charts to represent data visually.
- Keep the design clean and uncluttered, with plenty of whitespace.
- Ensure your branding is visible but not overpowering.

4. Videos

Video is one of the most powerful visual tools for enhancing your offer. It allows you to demonstrate your product in action, explain its benefits, or provide social proof through customer testimonials. Videos are also highly engaging, often resulting in higher conversion rates than static images or text alone.

Types of videos to consider:

- **Product demos**: Show how your product works, highlighting its key features.
- **Explainer videos**: Simplify complex ideas or processes in an engaging format.
- **Testimonial videos**: Feature satisfied customers sharing their experiences with your product or service.
- **Behind-the-scenes**: Offer a peek into your company's values, culture, or product creation process.

5. Icons and Graphics

Icons and custom graphics are versatile tools for simplifying information and making your offer visually appealing. They help break up text, guide the viewer's eye, and emphasize important points.

How to use icons effectively:

- Use icons to represent key benefits or features.
- Ensure the style of the icons matches your brand's design language.
- Use consistent colors and sizes to maintain visual harmony.

6. GIFs and Motion Graphics

Motion graphics and GIFs add a dynamic element to your visuals, making them more engaging. They can be used to showcase key product features, animate your logo, or guide the viewer's attention to important elements like CTAs.

Using GIFs and motion graphics:

- Use animation sparingly to avoid overwhelming the viewer.
- Highlight important moments, such as when a product is being used or a feature is being demonstrated.
- Ensure that the motion doesn't distract from your core message.

7. Social Proof Visuals

Visual social proof, such as user-generated content (UGC), customer testimonials, and case studies, enhances your offer by providing validation from real people. These visuals show prospective customers that others have benefited from your product or service, increasing trust and credibility.

Using social proof effectively:

- Include images of real customers using your product or service.
- Display customer quotes alongside their photos for a more personal touch.
- Use logos of well-known clients or publications to establish authority.

Key Takeaway:

There are many types of visuals that can enhance your offer, from product images and mockups to infographics, videos, and social proof. Choose the visual formats that best communicate the value of your offer and resonate with your audience.

4: Practical Tips for Creating Visuals

Now that you understand the types of visuals that can enhance your offer, it's time to dive into practical tips for creating or sourcing them. Whether you're working with a designer, using design tools yourself, or outsourcing to freelancers, these strategies will help ensure your visuals are effective and high-quality.

1. Choosing the Right Tools

There are many design tools available for creating professional visuals, even if you're not a designer. Here are some popular tools to consider:

- **Canva**: Canva is a user-friendly tool that allows you to create everything from social media graphics to presentations. It offers pre-made templates that you can customize with your brand colors and text.

- **Adobe Photoshop/Illustrator**: If you have more design experience, Adobe products are powerful tools for creating custom visuals. Photoshop is best for photo editing, while Illustrator is great for creating vector graphics.
- **Figma**: Figma is a collaborative design tool that's perfect for teams working together on digital products or marketing materials.
- **Loom**: For video content, Loom allows you to record quick product demos, walkthroughs, and testimonials with ease. It's ideal for creating explainer videos or sharing product features.

2. Working with Designers

If you don't have the time or expertise to create visuals yourself, working with a designer can help you achieve a professional look. Here's how to make the most of your collaboration:

- **Provide clear guidelines**: Share your brand's style guide, including colors, fonts, and any existing visual assets. Be clear about the goals of your visuals and the key messages you want to convey.
- **Use inspiration**: Share examples of visuals you like, whether from competitors or other brands, to give the designer a sense of your preferences.
- **Give constructive feedback**: Offer specific feedback on drafts, highlighting what you like and what needs improvement. Be respectful of

the designer's expertise while ensuring the final product aligns with your vision.

3. Outsourcing Visual Creation

If working with a full-time designer isn't feasible, you can outsource visual creation to freelancers or agencies. Platforms like **Upwork**, **Fiverr**, and **99designs** connect you with talented designers who can create high-quality visuals at an affordable price. When outsourcing, be sure to:

- Provide detailed project briefs that include your goals, brand guidelines, and visual preferences.
- Review portfolios and previous work to ensure the designer's style matches your vision.
- Establish clear deadlines and milestones to keep the project on track.

4. Optimizing Visuals for Different Platforms

Different platforms have unique requirements for visuals in terms of dimensions, file size, and formats. To ensure your visuals look great and perform well, follow these best practices:

- **Website and landing pages**: Use high-resolution images that load quickly by optimizing file size. Aim for JPG or PNG formats, and consider using WebP for faster loading times without compromising quality.
- **Social media**: Each social media platform has different image size recommendations. For example, Instagram uses square images (1080 x 1080 pixels), while Facebook and Twitter favor

landscape images. Make sure your visuals are tailored to the specific platform to ensure they display correctly.

- **Email marketing**: Optimize visuals for mobile and desktop views. Keep file sizes small to reduce loading times, and use alt text for images in case they don't load properly in email clients.

5. Tracking Visual Performance

To understand how your visuals are impacting your offer's success, track key performance metrics like engagement rates, click-through rates (CTR), and conversion rates. Use tools like **Google Analytics** for website traffic or **Facebook Insights** for social media to monitor the effectiveness of your visuals. If certain visuals consistently underperform, test different versions to see what resonates better with your audience.

Key Takeaway:

By using the right tools, collaborating with designers, and optimizing visuals for different platforms, you can create high-quality, impactful designs that enhance your offer and drive conversions.

Conclusion: Making Visuals Work for Your Offer

Visuals are a critical component of any successful offer. They help you grab attention, communicate value, and guide your audience through the decision-making process. From mastering design principles and selecting the right colors to choosing the best types of visuals for your offer, every decision you make about your visuals should serve to enhance your offer's appeal.

Remember that creating great visuals is both an art and a science. While it's important to focus on aesthetics, the ultimate goal of your visuals is to support the message and drive conversions. By using the strategies outlined in this chapter, you can create a visually compelling offer that resonates with your audience and enhances your brand's credibility.

By continuously testing and optimizing your visuals, you can ensure that they remain effective as your offer evolves and reaches new audiences. With the right approach, your visuals will not only attract attention but also drive the success of your irresistible offer.

Chapter 16

A/B TESTING YOUR OFFER

A/B testing is one of the most powerful tools in a marketer's toolkit for improving the performance of an offer. It allows you to systematically test different elements of your offer to determine which variations resonate most with your audience and drive the highest conversions. Whether you're testing headlines, images, pricing models, or call-to-action buttons, A/B testing helps take the guesswork out of optimization and gives you real data to back up your decisions.

This chapter will take you through the essentials of A/B testing, from the fundamentals of how it works to advanced strategies for maximizing your results. You'll learn the key elements to test, how to set up a successful experiment, and how to analyze your results to refine and optimize your offer.

1: Introduction to A/B Testing

What Is A/B Testing?

A/B testing, also known as split testing, is a method of comparing two versions of a web page, offer, or marketing asset to see which one performs better. By changing a single variable at a time and showing each version to a similar segment of your audience, you can determine which version drives more conversions, click-throughs, or other desired actions.

In a typical A/B test, "Version A" is the control (the original version), and "Version B" is a variation with one change. The version that delivers the better results is considered the winner, and those changes are implemented for the entire audience.

Why Is A/B Testing Important for Your Offer?

A/B testing is crucial because it removes the guesswork from marketing optimization. Without it, you might make changes to your offer based on assumptions or intuition that don't actually lead to better results. By running controlled experiments, you get real data on what works and what doesn't, allowing you to improve your conversion rates in a systematic way.

Benefits of A/B testing include:

- **Improved conversion rates**: By continuously testing and refining elements of your offer, you can significantly increase the percentage of people who convert into paying customers.
- **Better user experience**: Testing different layouts, messaging, or navigation options can help make your offer easier to understand and more user-friendly.
- **Data-driven decisions**: Rather than relying on opinions or assumptions, A/B testing provides concrete data to back up changes and optimizations.

- **Minimizing risk**: A/B testing allows you to make incremental changes and measure their impact before rolling them out to your entire audience, minimizing the risk of hurting your conversion rates.

How A/B Testing Works

A/B testing involves splitting your audience into two (or more) groups at random. One group is shown the control version of your offer, while the other is shown the variation. By comparing how each group responds—whether it's through clicks, purchases, or sign-ups—you can determine which version performs better.

The basic process of A/B testing includes:

1. **Identify the variable**: Choose one element of your offer to test (such as the headline, image, or CTA).
2. **Create two versions**: Create a variation that differs from your control version in only one way.
3. **Split your audience**: Use A/B testing software to randomly split your audience into two groups.
4. **Run the test**: Allow the test to run long enough to gather sufficient data for statistical significance.
5. **Analyze the results**: Determine which version performed better based on key metrics, such as conversion rate.
6. **Implement changes**: Apply the winning variation to your offer, and consider testing further to continue optimizing.

Key Takeaway:

A/B testing is a data-driven approach to optimizing your offer by systematically testing variations and measuring their impact on conversion rates. By running controlled experiments, you can make informed decisions that improve the performance of your offer.

2: Key Elements to Test in Your Offer

1. Headlines

The headline is often the first thing a visitor sees, and it plays a crucial role in grabbing attention and drawing people into your offer. Testing different headlines can help you identify which messaging resonates most with your audience and drives more clicks or sign-ups.

What to Test:

- **Headline length**: Short, punchy headlines vs. longer, more detailed ones.
- **Tone**: Casual vs. formal language.
- **Value proposition**: Focusing on different benefits (e.g., "Save time with our tool" vs. "Get the best results with our tool").
- **Emotional triggers**: Headlines that evoke curiosity, urgency, or excitement.

Example:

- **Version A**: "Boost Your Productivity with Our Simple Time Management Tool"
- **Version B**: "Cut Your Workday in Half with Our Time Management Software"

2. Call-to-Action (CTA) Buttons

CTAs are critical because they prompt the user to take the desired action, whether it's signing up, making a purchase, or downloading a resource. Small tweaks to your CTA buttons can lead to significant improvements in conversion rates.

What to Test:

- **Button text**: Action-oriented vs. benefit-focused (e.g., "Sign Up Now" vs. "Get Your Free Trial").
- **Color**: Different colors can affect how much the button stands out on the page.
- **Size and placement**: Larger buttons or buttons placed higher up on the page may result in higher conversions.
- **Urgency language**: Adding urgency (e.g., "Buy Now—Limited Time Offer") vs. neutral language (e.g., "Learn More").

Example:

- **Version A**: "Start Your Free Trial"
- **Version B**: "Claim Your 30-Day Free Trial"

3. Product Descriptions

The way you describe your product or service has a direct impact on how your audience perceives its value. Testing different approaches to product descriptions can help you find the one that converts best.

What to Test:

- **Length**: Short vs. detailed descriptions.
- **Format**: Bulleted lists vs. paragraphs.
- **Focus**: Feature-focused vs. benefit-focused messaging.

- **Storytelling**: Incorporating a story into the product description to make it more relatable.

Example:

- **Version A**: "Our project management tool helps you stay organized with powerful task tracking features."
- **Version B**: "Tired of losing track of tasks? Our tool helps you stay on top of your workload with an easy-to-use task tracker."

4. Pricing and Payment Plans

Pricing can be a significant deciding factor for potential customers. A/B testing different pricing models, discounts, or payment plans can help you find the structure that drives the most sales.

What to Test:

- **Price points**: Testing different price levels to find the optimal balance between value and affordability.
- **Discounts**: Offering limited-time discounts, bundling products, or offering coupon codes.
- **Payment plans**: Offering monthly vs. annual payment options, or single-payment vs. subscription models.
- **Framing**: Highlighting different pricing options or presenting the savings from annual plans.

Example:

- **Version A**: "$29 per month"
- **Version B**: "$290 per year (Save 20%)"

5. Images and Visuals

Images and visuals are essential in shaping how potential customers perceive your offer. Testing different images, product shots, or illustrations can significantly impact user engagement and conversion rates.

What to Test:

- **Hero image**: Different hero images (e.g., lifestyle images vs. product images).
- **Product photos**: Testing various angles or close-ups of your product.
- **Illustrations vs. photos**: Using custom illustrations to explain concepts vs. using stock photos.
- **Colors and styles**: Testing different color schemes for your offer page.

Example:

- **Version A**: A lifestyle image of a person using your product.
- **Version B**: A close-up shot of the product itself.

6. Form Length and Fields

If your offer requires users to fill out a form (for sign-ups, downloads, or purchases), the form's length and complexity can significantly affect conversion rates. Testing different form variations can help reduce friction and improve completion rates.

What to Test:

- **Number of fields**: Reducing the number of fields to minimize effort.

- **Optional vs. required fields**: Making certain fields optional to see if it impacts completion.
- **Form layout**: Horizontal vs. vertical alignment, multi-step vs. single-step forms.
- **Placeholder text**: Using guiding text in form fields to help users fill them out faster.

Example:

- **Version A**: 5-field form (Name, Email, Phone, Company, Job Title)
- **Version B**: 3-field form (Name, Email, Phone)

7. Testimonials and Social Proof

Social proof, such as customer testimonials or reviews, can be highly persuasive. Testing how and where you display testimonials can help you identify the most effective approach to building trust.

What to Test:

- **Number of testimonials**: A single powerful testimonial vs. multiple shorter ones.
- **Placement**: Testimonials at the top of the page vs. at the bottom.
- **Format**: Text-based testimonials vs. video testimonials.
- **Specificity**: Vague, generalized testimonials vs. detailed testimonials with specific results.

Example:

- **Version A**: "John increased his productivity by 50% using our tool!"

- **Version B**: "Our team finished projects 2x faster after implementing this software."

8. Trust Badges and Guarantees

Trust badges (like security certifications or awards) and guarantees (like money-back guarantees) can alleviate concerns and encourage customers to take the next step. Testing different badges or guarantees can help you determine which boosts conversion the most.

What to Test:

- **Type of badge**: Security badges (SSL, Secure Checkout) vs. industry awards (Top Rated by XYZ).
- **Guarantee length**: A 30-day money-back guarantee vs. a 60-day guarantee.
- **Placement**: Badges at the checkout stage vs. earlier in the funnel.
- **Guarantee messaging**: Highlighting "risk-free" or "hassle-free" guarantees.

Example:

- **Version A**: "100% Money-Back Guarantee for 30 Days"
- **Version B**: "60-Day Hassle-Free Money-Back Guarantee"

Key Takeaway:

There are many elements of your offer that you can test, from headlines and CTA buttons to product descriptions and pricing models. By systematically testing these elements, you can continuously optimize your offer for better conversions and performance.

3: Setting Up an Effective A/B Test

Step 1: Define Your Objective

Before setting up an A/B test, you need to be clear about what you're trying to achieve. What's the specific metric you want to improve? Common objectives include:

- **Increasing conversion rates**: More sign-ups, purchases, or downloads.
- **Improving engagement**: More time spent on page, clicks, or shares.
- **Reducing bounce rates**: Keeping visitors on your offer page longer.

Choose one objective per test to keep the focus clear and measure success accurately.

Step 2: Choose One Variable to Test

A successful A/B test isolates one variable at a time. This allows you to determine exactly which change led to the improvement. Testing multiple variables at once can confuse the results and make it harder to identify which element was responsible for the change.

For example, if you're testing two different CTA buttons, keep the rest of the page identical. If you change both the CTA button and the headline, it's unclear which change drove the results.

Step 3: Create Two Versions of Your Offer

After deciding which element to test, create two versions of your offer: the control (Version A) and the variation (Version B). Make sure that Version B is identical to Version A except for the one element you are testing.

Example:

- **Version A**: "Get Your Free Guide Today!"
- **Version B**: "Download Your Free eBook Now!"

Step 4: Split Your Audience

To get accurate and reliable results, you need to split your audience evenly and randomly. This ensures that each version of your offer is shown to a representative sample of your total audience. Most A/B testing tools (such as Google Optimize, Optimizely, or VWO) can automatically divide your traffic evenly between the control and variation.

Step 5: Run the Test for a Sufficient Time Period

One of the most common mistakes in A/B testing is ending the test too early. You need to collect enough data to ensure that your results are statistically significant. If your audience is small, you may need to run the test for several days or weeks to get reliable results.

Determining Sample Size

To ensure your test results are valid, you need to calculate the sample size required for statistical significance. This depends on factors like the expected change in conversion rate and the amount of traffic you receive. Many A/B testing platforms have built-in calculators that can help you estimate the sample size needed for your test.

Step 6: Analyze the Results

Once the test has been running long enough to gather sufficient data, it's time to analyze the results. Compare the performance of Version A and Version B based on your chosen objective. If Version B outperforms the control, you've found a winner.

Key Metrics to Monitor:

- **Conversion Rate**: The percentage of visitors who complete the desired action (e.g., sign up, purchase).
- **Click-Through Rate (CTR)**: The percentage of visitors who click on your CTA button or link.
- **Bounce Rate**: The percentage of visitors who leave your page without taking any action.

If the results show that one version performs significantly better, you can implement that variation as the new control. If the test results are inconclusive, consider testing a different variation or running the test for a longer period.

Step 7: Rinse and Repeat

A/B testing is not a one-time activity—it's an ongoing process. Once you've found a winning variation, consider testing other elements of your offer. Continuous testing allows you to make incremental improvements that add up to significant gains in conversion rates over time.

Key Takeaway:

Setting up an A/B test involves defining clear objectives, testing one variable at a time, running the test long enough to gather reliable data, and analyzing the results to determine the winner. Continuous testing allows you to make data-driven decisions that lead to ongoing improvements.

4: Advanced A/B Testing Strategies

Once you've mastered the basics of A/B testing, you can move on to more advanced strategies to further optimize your offer and maximize your results. These strategies include multivariate testing, testing multiple offers, and personalization.

Multivariate Testing

Multivariate testing takes A/B testing to the next level by allowing you to test multiple elements of your offer at once. Rather than just testing one variable (like the headline or CTA), you can test several variables in combination to see which combination performs best.

Example: If you're testing both a new headline and a new CTA button, a multivariate test would create four versions:

1. Version A: Original headline, original CTA
2. Version B: Original headline, new CTA
3. Version C: New headline, original CTA
4. Version D: New headline, new CTA

Multivariate testing allows you to see how different elements interact with each other and which combination leads to the best results. However, it requires more traffic than a simple A/B test because there are more variations to test.

Sequential Testing

Sequential testing involves running a series of A/B tests, with each test building on the results of the previous one. This allows you to make small, incremental improvements over time rather than testing large changes all at once.

Example: First, you test two different headlines. Once you've found a winner, you move on to testing different CTA buttons. After that, you test different images. By testing each element in sequence, you can systematically optimize every aspect of your offer.

Personalization in A/B Testing

Another advanced strategy is to incorporate personalization into your A/B testing. Instead of testing a single variation for your entire audience, you can segment your audience and test different variations for each segment.

Example: You might run one version of your offer for first-time visitors and another version for returning customers. By personalizing your offer based on the audience segment, you can increase relevance and improve conversion rates.

Testing Multiple Offers

If you have more than one offer, you can use A/B testing to determine which offer resonates best with your audience.

This is particularly useful if you're testing different value propositions or pricing models.

Example:

- **Version A**: "Get 20% Off Your First Purchase"
- **Version B**: "Buy One, Get One Free"

By testing different offers, you can see which one generates the most conversions and build your marketing strategy around that winning offer.

Key Takeaway:

Advanced A/B testing strategies like multivariate testing, sequential testing, and personalization allow you to take your optimization efforts to the next level. By testing multiple elements or offers at once, you can gain deeper insights into what drives conversions and continuously improve your offer.

5: Analyzing and Interpreting A/B Test Results

Statistical Significance

One of the most important aspects of analyzing A/B test results is determining whether the differences between Version A and Version B are statistically significant. Statistical significance means that the results are unlikely to have occurred by chance and that you can confidently attribute the difference in performance to the change you made.

P-Values and Confidence Levels

Most A/B testing tools will provide a p-value or confidence level along with your results. A p-value of 0.05 (or a 95% confidence level) is the standard threshold for statistical significance. This means that there's only a 5% chance that the results are due to random variation, making the results reliable.

Key Metrics to Focus On

When analyzing your A/B test results, it's essential to focus on the right metrics. Depending on your objective, you may look at different KPIs to determine success.

1. **Conversion Rate**: This is the most critical metric for most A/B tests. It measures the percentage of visitors who complete the desired action (e.g., making a purchase, signing up for a newsletter, downloading an eBook).
2. **Click-Through Rate (CTR)**: For tests involving links, buttons, or CTAs, the CTR tells you how many people clicked on the element relative to the total number of viewers.
3. **Bounce Rate**: A high bounce rate indicates that visitors are leaving your page without taking action. Reducing the bounce rate often leads to higher conversions.
4. **Time on Page**: If one version of your offer page keeps visitors engaged longer than the other, it may suggest that the messaging or layout is more compelling.

5. **Revenue per Visitor (RPV)**: For eCommerce businesses, RPV helps you measure the total revenue generated per visitor. This metric can provide deeper insights into how your offer impacts overall revenue.

Avoiding Common A/B Testing Pitfalls

To get the most out of your A/B testing efforts, it's essential to avoid common mistakes that can skew your results or lead to inaccurate conclusions.

1. Ending the Test Too Early

One of the most common mistakes is ending a test before it has reached statistical significance. If you don't have enough data, the results may be due to random chance rather than an actual difference between Version A and Version B. Always let your test run long enough to gather sufficient data.

2. Testing Too Many Variables at Once

Testing multiple variables at the same time can make it difficult to pinpoint what caused the change in performance. If you want accurate results, focus on one element per test. If you're testing multiple elements, consider using a multivariate test instead of a simple A/B test.

3. Ignoring External Factors

Sometimes, external factors (such as holidays, major news events, or seasonal trends) can impact the results of your A/B test. Be mindful of the context in which your test is running, and consider re-running the test at a different time if necessary.

4. Misinterpreting Results

It's important to interpret your results in the context of your overall marketing strategy. Just because one variation performs better in a test doesn't necessarily mean it's the best choice for your long-term goals. Consider how the results align with your broader business objectives before making changes.

Acting on A/B Test Results

Once you've analyzed your test results, it's time to take action. If one version outperformed the other, implement the winning variation and monitor its impact over time. Remember that A/B testing is an ongoing process, so once you've found a winner, you can move on to testing other elements to continue optimizing your offer.

Key Takeaway:

Analyzing your A/B test results requires careful attention to statistical significance, key metrics, and potential external factors. By avoiding common pitfalls and interpreting your results in context, you can make data-driven decisions that lead to meaningful improvements in your offer's performance.

Conclusion: The Power of Continuous A/B Testing

A/B testing is a powerful tool that allows you to optimize your offer based on real data, rather than guesswork or assumptions. By testing different elements of your offer—such as headlines, CTAs, images, pricing, and product descriptions—you can systematically improve conversion rates and overall performance.

The key to success with A/B testing is consistency. It's not enough to run a single test and move on. Continuous testing allows you to make incremental improvements that add up over time, helping you stay ahead of the competition and meet the evolving needs of your audience.

Final Key Takeaways:

1. **Test One Element at a Time**: Focus on testing a single variable to get clear, actionable results.
2. **Run Tests Long Enough for Statistical Significance**: Patience is key—make sure you have enough data before drawing conclusions.
3. **Track the Right Metrics**: Depending on your objective, focus on conversion rates, CTR, bounce rates, or revenue per visitor to measure success.
4. **Learn and Iterate**: Use your test results to make informed decisions, but continue testing to refine and optimize your offer over time.

Looking Ahead

A/B testing is not just a one-time experiment; it's an ongoing strategy for growth. As you continue to test and optimize your offer, you'll gain deeper insights into what resonates with your audience and what drives the best results. This data-driven approach will not only improve the effectiveness of your current offer but also set you up for long-term success as you refine and scale your business.

By mastering the art of A/B testing, you'll be better equipped to create offers that truly connect with your audience, drive conversions, and ultimately dominate your market.

Chapter 17

CREATING MULTI-CHANNEL MARKETING CAMPAIGNS

Customers are engaging with brands across numerous platforms and touchpoints, from social media and email to search engines and display ads. As a result, businesses must meet their audience where they are and provide a seamless experience across multiple channels. This is where multi-channel marketing comes into play. Multi-channel marketing allows you to promote your offers and brand through various platforms, engaging your audience in a more comprehensive and effective way.

In this chapter, we'll cover everything you need to know about creating multi-channel marketing campaigns that capture attention, build brand awareness, and drive conversions. We'll explore how to choose the right channels, coordinate your message across platforms, measure performance, and refine your campaigns for maximum impact.

1: What is Multi-Channel Marketing?

Defining Multi-Channel Marketing

Multi-channel marketing refers to the practice of interacting with customers through various communication channels, both online and offline, to create a cohesive and engaging experience. Rather than relying on a single platform (such as email or social media), a multi-channel strategy leverages a mix of mediums to reach and engage with your target audience.

These channels can include:

- **Digital Channels**: Social media, email, search engines (SEO and PPC), display ads, websites, and mobile apps.
- **Traditional Channels**: Direct mail, TV, radio, print ads, and in-store marketing.

Why Multi-Channel Marketing Matters

Customers today don't just use one platform to engage with brands—they use multiple. They might discover your product through a Google search, follow you on Instagram, and finally make a purchase after receiving a targeted email. A multi-channel approach ensures that your brand stays top-of-mind, no matter how or where your audience is interacting with you.

Key benefits of multi-channel marketing include:

- **Increased visibility**: By being present across various channels, you increase the chances of reaching your target audience.

- **Better customer engagement**: Different customers prefer different platforms, so using multiple channels ensures you meet them where they feel most comfortable.
- **Improved conversion rates**: A coordinated presence across several touchpoints can guide customers through the buying journey, increasing the likelihood of conversion.
- **Greater customer insights**: Multi-channel marketing allows you to gather data from various sources, providing deeper insights into customer behavior.

Omnichannel vs. Multi-Channel

While multi-channel marketing involves using multiple channels, omnichannel marketing takes it a step further by integrating those channels into a seamless experience. In omnichannel marketing, the customer's interactions across various platforms (e.g., browsing on mobile, visiting a physical store, and receiving email) are all interconnected, providing a cohesive journey.

In this chapter, we will focus on the foundation of multi-channel marketing, with the understanding that creating a seamless, omnichannel experience is the next level of sophistication in marketing strategy.

2: Choosing the Right Marketing Channels

Understanding Your Audience

The first step in creating a successful multi-channel marketing campaign is understanding your audience.

Different customer segments interact with brands in different ways, and not every channel will be right for every business. Before choosing your channels, conduct thorough research on where your audience spends their time and how they prefer to engage with content.

Here are a few ways to gather insights about your audience:

- **Customer surveys**: Ask your current customers where they spend most of their time online, how they discovered your brand, and what channels they use for shopping or entertainment.
- **Analytics tools**: Use tools like Google Analytics, Facebook Insights, or Instagram Analytics to track which platforms are driving the most traffic and engagement.
- **Competitor research**: Look at how your competitors are using different channels and assess which platforms appear to be driving the most success.

Aligning Channels with Your Business Goals

Once you understand your audience, the next step is to align your channels with your business objectives. Different channels are better suited for different goals. For example:

- **Brand awareness**: Social media platforms like Instagram, Facebook, and YouTube are excellent for building brand awareness, especially through engaging visual content.
- **Lead generation**: Search engines (via SEO and PPC), email marketing, and paid social ads are

effective for driving traffic to landing pages and capturing leads.

- **Conversions and sales**: Email marketing, retargeting ads, and direct response advertising are highly effective at converting leads into paying customers.
- **Customer retention**: Loyalty programs, email newsletters, and personalized offers can be distributed through multiple channels to keep customers engaged.

Key Marketing Channels

Here's an overview of some of the most effective digital marketing channels and how they can be integrated into a multi-channel strategy:

1. Social Media

Social media platforms such as Facebook, Instagram, LinkedIn, TikTok, and Twitter are essential for building brand awareness and engaging with your audience. Each platform has its own strengths:

- **Facebook**: Great for targeted ads, especially for older demographics.
- **Instagram**: Visual platform ideal for branding and showcasing products.
- **LinkedIn**: Best for B2B marketing and reaching professionals.
- **TikTok**: A platform for engaging with younger audiences through short-form video content.
- **Twitter**: Great for real-time communication and customer service.

2. Email Marketing

Email is one of the most powerful channels for nurturing leads and driving conversions. Email allows for highly personalized communication and can be automated to guide customers through the funnel.

3. Search Engines (SEO and PPC)

Search engine optimization (SEO) helps you rank organically on search engines like Google, driving long-term traffic to your website. Pay-per-click (PPC) advertising, such as Google Ads, allows you to target specific keywords and drive immediate traffic to landing pages.

4. Content Marketing

Content marketing, including blog posts, videos, podcasts, and infographics, is key to educating your audience and building trust over time. Content can be shared across multiple platforms, from your website and email campaigns to social media and YouTube.

5. Display Advertising and Retargeting

Display ads appear across the web on various websites, often as banners, videos, or interactive ads. Retargeting ads show your content to users who have already visited your website or engaged with your brand, helping bring them back for another interaction.

6. Mobile Marketing

With a growing percentage of users accessing content on mobile devices, mobile marketing has become essential.

This includes mobile apps, SMS marketing, and push notifications.

Key Takeaway:

Choosing the right marketing channels depends on your audience's behavior and your business goals. By understanding which platforms align with your objectives, you can effectively allocate resources to the channels that will provide the best ROI.

3: Creating Consistent Messaging Across Channels

The Importance of Consistent Messaging

Consistency is key in multi-channel marketing. While your audience may engage with your brand on different platforms, the message and experience should remain consistent. Inconsistent messaging can confuse potential customers, dilute your brand, and ultimately hurt conversions.

Elements of Consistent Messaging:

- **Brand voice**: Your brand should sound the same across all platforms, whether it's on social media, in an email, or on your website. Define your brand's tone and ensure that all copywriters and marketers adhere to It.
- **Visual identity**: Your brand's colors, fonts, logos, and overall visual style should be consistent across all marketing materials.

- **Value proposition**: The core message of your offer should remain the same across channels, even if it's tailored for different audiences or formats.
- **CTAs (Calls to Action)**: Use consistent calls to action across channels to reinforce the desired next step in the customer journey, whether it's signing up for a newsletter, making a purchase, or downloading a free resource.

Customizing Content for Different Platforms

While consistency is essential, each platform requires slightly different content formats and engagement strategies. The goal is to adapt your core message to suit each channel without changing its essence.

Here's how to customize your content for different platforms while maintaining a unified message:

1. Social Media

Social media platforms are ideal for quick, engaging content that encourages interaction. The content here is often shorter and more visually driven.

- **Instagram**: Focus on high-quality visuals and short captions. Use Instagram Stories and Reels to deliver more informal, behind-the-scenes content.
- **LinkedIn**: Publish thought leadership content and case studies that are more in-depth and formal.
- **Facebook**: Combine a mix of visuals, videos, and text to tell stories or promote offers.
- **TikTok**: Create fun, engaging, and visually captivating short-form videos with clear calls to action.

2. Email

Email allows for more direct, personalized communication. You can use email to dive deeper into your offers and nurture relationships with detailed content such as:

- Welcome series for new subscribers.
- Product promotions with personalized recommendations.
- Newsletters with a mix of educational content and offers.

3. Website and SEO Content

Your website is your central hub for information. Use long-form content, such as blog posts, eBooks, and whitepapers, to provide valuable insights and educational resources that build trust. Optimize these pieces for SEO to attract organic traffic.

4. Paid Ads

Paid advertising—whether on social media or search engines—should be direct, attention-grabbing, and clear. While ads need to stand out, they should still align with your brand's overall messaging. Keep the copy concise and focus on compelling visuals and clear CTAs.

Cohesive Campaign Example: Seasonal Sale

To illustrate, imagine you're launching a seasonal sale for an eCommerce store. Your consistent messaging across channels might look like this:

- **Instagram/Facebook**: Post visually engaging product shots with "20% Off Summer Sale" as the main message, and include a link to your website.

- **Email Campaign**: Send targeted emails to your list, highlighting the same sale with product recommendations tailored to past purchases.
- **Google Ads**: Run search and display ads with the same "20% Off Summer Sale" message, targeting users who have previously visited your website or searched for related items.
- **Website**: Feature a prominent banner on the homepage with a countdown timer creating urgency for the sale's end date.

While each platform has its nuances, the core message—your seasonal sale—remains the same, and the visual branding stays consistent across all channels.

Key Takeaway:

Consistency across channels is essential for creating a cohesive brand experience. While each platform has different content requirements, the messaging, visual identity, and calls to action should align to reinforce your offer.

4: Integrating Paid and Organic Strategies

Balancing Paid and Organic Tactics

An effective multi-channel marketing campaign often combines both paid and organic strategies. Each has its own strengths, and when used together, they can maximize your reach and impact.

Paid Channels

- **Social Media Ads**: Paid social ads allow you to reach highly targeted audiences based on demographics, interests, and behaviors. Use paid ads to drive traffic to your landing pages, products, or lead magnets.
- **Search Ads (PPC)**: With search ads, you can target users who are actively searching for terms related to your product or service, driving highly qualified traffic to your website.
- **Display Ads**: Display ads help raise awareness and retarget users who have visited your website but haven't converted yet.

Organic Channels

- **SEO and Content Marketing**: Organic traffic from SEO and content marketing builds authority over time. A consistent blog, video series, or podcast can establish your brand as an expert in your industry, driving long-term traffic without ongoing ad spend.
- **Social Media Content**: Regular posting on social media helps engage followers, build community, and increase brand visibility without the need for paid ads.

Using Retargeting to Combine Paid and Organic Strategies

Retargeting ads are a powerful way to bring back users who have engaged with your organic content but haven't yet converted. For example, someone who reads your blog post might later see a retargeting ad on Facebook or Google, reminding them of your product or offer.

Example of a Retargeting Campaign:

- **Step 1**: Publish an SEO-optimized blog post that attracts organic traffic to your website.
- **Step 2**: Use Facebook or Google retargeting ads to target visitors who spent time on that blog post but didn't take action.
- **Step 3**: Serve them a targeted ad highlighting your lead magnet, special offer, or product with a strong CTA to bring them back.

This combination of organic and paid efforts ensures that you're maximizing the value of your content while also driving conversions through retargeting.

Tracking the Effectiveness of Paid and Organic Channels

To ensure your paid and organic efforts are working together effectively, it's important to track the performance of each channel. Tools like Google Analytics, UTM tracking codes, and social media insights allow you to monitor traffic, conversions, and ROI across different platforms.

- **Organic metrics**: Track organic traffic, keyword rankings, social media engagement, and time spent on content.
- **Paid metrics**: Monitor click-through rates (CTR), cost per acquisition (CPA), and conversion rates for your paid campaigns.

Key Takeaway:

Integrating paid and organic strategies is essential for maximizing the reach of your multi-channel campaigns. Paid tactics provide immediate traffic and conversions, while organic efforts build long-term visibility and engagement. Combining both strategies allows you to create a well-rounded marketing campaign that drives results.

5: Measuring Success Across Channels

Setting Goals and KPIs

To measure the success of a multi-channel marketing campaign, you need to define clear goals and key performance indicators (KPIs). Your KPIs will depend on the specific objectives of your campaign, such as increasing brand awareness, driving traffic, generating leads, or boosting conversions.

Examples of KPIs for Different Goals:

- **Brand awareness**: Impressions, reach, and social media followers.
- **Traffic generation**: Website traffic, click-through rates (CTR), and time spent on the site.
- **Lead generation**: Number of leads captured, conversion rates, and cost per lead (CPL).
- **Sales and conversions**: Number of sales, revenue, average order value (AOV), and return on ad spend (ROAS).

Tracking Across Multiple Platforms

Because multi-channel marketing involves several platforms, you'll need a comprehensive system for tracking performance. Here are some of the most commonly used tools for measuring campaign success:

1. Google Analytics

Google Analytics allows you to track website traffic, user behavior, and conversions. You can segment traffic by source (organic search, social media, email, paid ads) to see how each channel contributes to overall performance.

2. Social Media Insights

Platforms like Facebook, Instagram, and LinkedIn provide built-in analytics that show how well your posts, ads, and profiles are performing. Track engagement, reach, and follower growth to evaluate the effectiveness of your social media efforts.

3. Email Marketing Tools

Email platforms such as Mailchimp, ActiveCampaign, and HubSpot provide detailed reports on open rates, click-through rates, and conversion rates. These insights help you understand how email marketing contributes to your overall campaign performance.

4. Ad Platforms

Both Google Ads and social media ad platforms provide metrics such as click-through rate (CTR), cost per click (CPC), and conversion rates. These metrics allow you to monitor the ROI of your paid campaigns.

Multi-Touch Attribution

One of the challenges of multi-channel marketing is accurately attributing conversions to the right channel. Multi-touch attribution models help solve this problem by assigning credit to all the touchpoints that contributed to a sale or conversion.

Attribution Models:

- **Last-click attribution**: All credit is given to the final touchpoint before the conversion.
- **First-click attribution**: All credit is given to the first interaction a customer had with your brand.
- **Linear attribution**: Credit is evenly distributed across all touchpoints in the customer journey.
- **Time decay attribution**: Touchpoints closer to the conversion receive more credit than earlier interactions.

By using multi-touch attribution, you can get a more accurate understanding of how your various channels work together to drive conversions.

Key Takeaway:

Tracking the success of a multi-channel campaign requires clear goals, defined KPIs, and the right tools for monitoring performance across platforms. Multi-touch attribution helps you understand how different channels contribute to overall success, enabling you to refine your strategy for better results.

6: Refining Your Multi-Channel Campaigns

Analyzing Data and Making Adjustments

Once you've gathered data on the performance of your campaign, it's time to analyze the results and make adjustments. Look for patterns in which channels are driving the most engagement, traffic, and conversions, and optimize your efforts accordingly.

Key Questions to Ask:

- Which channels are driving the most conversions?
- Are there any underperforming channels that need adjustment?
- What content is resonating most with your audience?
- How are different customer segments responding to your campaigns?

Optimizing Underperforming Channels

If certain channels aren't performing as expected, consider the following strategies for improvement:

- **Content adjustments**: Refine the messaging, visuals, or format of the content you're using on that channel.
- **Targeting improvements**: Adjust your audience targeting to ensure you're reaching the right people.
- **Frequency adjustments**: Experiment with increasing or decreasing the frequency of your posts, emails, or ads.

Scaling Your Best-Performing Channels

Once you've identified which channels are delivering the best results, consider allocating more budget or resources to those areas. Scaling successful channels allows you to amplify what's working and drive even more conversions.

Example:

If Facebook ads are driving the majority of your leads, consider increasing your ad spend or testing new ad formats (such as carousel ads or video ads) to maximize your results.

Testing and Iterating

Multi-channel marketing is an ongoing process of testing, learning, and optimizing. Continuously test new strategies, audiences, and content formats to keep improving your results. Consider A/B testing different versions of ads, emails, or landing pages to determine which performs better.

Continuous Improvement:

- **Test new messaging**: Experiment with different value propositions, CTAs, or offers.
- **Refine audience segments**: Test different customer segments to see if certain groups respond better to specific channels.
- **Try new platforms**: Stay up-to-date with emerging channels (such as TikTok or Clubhouse) and test them to see if they align with your audience.

Key Takeaway:

Refining your multi-channel campaigns is essential for ongoing success. By analyzing data, optimizing underperforming channels, scaling successful ones, and continuously testing new ideas, you can improve your results and ensure that your marketing efforts stay effective over time.

Conclusion: Building a Successful Multi-Channel Marketing Strategy

Creating a multi-channel marketing campaign is a powerful way to reach your audience, build brand awareness, and drive conversions across multiple platforms. By understanding your audience, choosing the right channels, maintaining consistent messaging, and integrating paid and organic strategies, you can create a cohesive campaign that delivers results.

Final Key Takeaways:

1. **Understand Your Audience**: Research your audience's behavior and preferences to choose the right mix of channels for your campaign.
2. **Create Consistent Messaging**: Ensure that your brand voice, visual identity, and core message are consistent across all platforms, even as you tailor content for each channel's unique format.
3. **Balance Paid and Organic Efforts**: Use both paid and organic strategies to maximize reach, engagement, and conversions, and use retargeting to bring back warm leads.

4. **Track and Measure Performance**: Use analytics tools to monitor the performance of each channel, and apply multi-touch attribution to understand how different touchpoints contribute to conversions.
5. **Refine and Optimize**: Continuously analyze data, test new ideas, and optimize your campaigns for better performance.

By following these strategies, you can create effective multi-channel marketing campaigns that resonate with your audience, drive meaningful engagement, and boost your business's bottom line.

Chapter 18

THE ROLE OF AUTOMATION IN SCALING OFFERS

Scaling an irresistible offer is one of the most critical phases for growing a business. Whether you're offering a product, service, or digital solution, scaling your offer effectively means reaching more customers, increasing conversions, and maintaining high operational efficiency. However, scaling comes with its own set of challenges—handling increased demand, managing customer relationships, and streamlining workflows can become overwhelming without the right tools and strategies in place.

This is where automation plays a transformative role. Automation enables you to manage repetitive tasks, personalize customer interactions, optimize marketing and sales processes, and streamline operations. By implementing automation strategically, businesses can scale their offers more efficiently and sustainably, all while maintaining a personalized customer experience.

This chapter will explore the role of automation in scaling offers, including key areas to automate, tools and technologies available, best practices for implementation, and real-world examples of businesses successfully leveraging automation to scale their offers.

1: Understanding Automation and Its Importance in Scaling Offers

What is Automation?

Automation refers to the use of technology to perform tasks and processes with minimal human intervention. In the context of scaling offers, automation involves streamlining workflows, marketing, sales, customer service, and operational tasks to handle increasing customer demand without overwhelming resources.

Automation can take many forms, including:

- **Marketing automation**: Automating email campaigns, lead nurturing, social media posts, and customer segmentation.
- **Sales automation**: Automating repetitive sales tasks, such as lead scoring, CRM updates, and follow-ups.
- **Customer service automation**: Using chatbots, automated ticketing systems, and self-service options for customer inquiries.
- **Operational automation**: Streamlining inventory management, order fulfillment, billing, and reporting.

Why Automation is Critical for Scaling Offers

As your business grows, so does the complexity of managing an increasing number of customers, orders, and transactions. Scaling manually is inefficient and costly.

Automation allows you to handle increased volume while minimizing errors, reducing costs, and maintaining a consistent level of service. Here are some key reasons why automation is critical for scaling:

1. **Efficiency**: Automation enables you to manage more tasks with fewer resources, allowing your team to focus on higher-value activities like strategy and customer relationship building.
2. **Consistency**: Automated processes ensure that tasks are carried out consistently and according to predefined rules, reducing the risk of human error and improving customer experience.
3. **Speed**: Automation accelerates processes, from lead generation and follow-ups to order processing and customer support, helping you keep up with demand and respond to customers faster.
4. **Cost-effectiveness**: By reducing the need for manual labor, automation lowers operational costs and allows you to scale your offer without exponentially increasing overhead.
5. **Data-driven insights**: Automated systems provide valuable data on customer behavior, sales trends, and marketing performance, enabling better decision-making and optimization.

Key Takeaway:

Automation is essential for scaling offers because it boosts efficiency, consistency, and speed while reducing operational costs. By automating key processes, businesses can scale sustainably without sacrificing quality or customer experience.

2: Automating Lead Generation and Nurturing

Automating Lead Generation

Lead generation is one of the most critical components of scaling an offer. To scale effectively, you need to continuously attract new leads while ensuring that the process of capturing and managing those leads is as streamlined as possible. Automation tools help you reach, capture, and qualify leads more efficiently by eliminating manual tasks.

Key Automation Tools for Lead Generation:

- **Forms and Pop-ups**: Automated lead capture forms, exit-intent pop-ups, and landing page forms collect leads 24/7, even when your team is offline. Tools like OptinMonster and Hello Bar help you create targeted pop-ups based on user behavior.
- **Chatbots**: Chatbots like Drift and Intercom engage website visitors in real-time, answering questions, providing recommendations, and capturing lead information for further nurturing.
- **Automated Ads**: Platforms like Google Ads and Facebook Ads offer automation features like dynamic ad targeting, audience segmentation, and budget optimization. Automated bidding ensures that your ad spend is optimized for the best possible return on investment.

Example Workflow:

1. A visitor arrives at your website and is shown a pop-up offering a free resource (e.g., an eBook or webinar).

2. The visitor enters their email address, triggering an automated email sequence (see next section).
3. If the visitor engages with the chatbot, their responses are captured and used to tailor the next steps in the lead nurturing process.

Automating Lead Nurturing

Once you've captured leads, nurturing them through automated email marketing and personalized follow-ups is essential to guide them through the customer journey. Lead nurturing automation ensures that each prospect receives timely, relevant content based on their interests and behaviors, all without manual intervention.

Key Automation Tools for Lead Nurturing:

- **Email Automation**: Platforms like Mailchimp, ActiveCampaign, and HubSpot allow you to set up drip campaigns, personalized email sequences, and behavior-triggered emails. These tools help nurture leads based on specific actions (e.g., email opens, link clicks, or product page visits).
- **Dynamic Content**: Tools like Marketo and ActiveCampaign allow you to create dynamic, personalized email content based on customer preferences, purchase history, or website activity. For example, if a lead downloads an eBook on a specific topic, future emails can focus on related content or products.
- **Lead Scoring**: Lead scoring tools like Pardot and Salesforce assign scores to leads based on their interactions with your content, emails, and

website. When a lead reaches a certain score, they can be automatically passed to the sales team for follow-up.

Example Workflow:

1. A lead downloads a whitepaper from your website, triggering an automated email sequence that delivers relevant follow-up content.
2. The lead opens one of the emails and clicks a link to view a product demo, increasing their lead score.
3. Once the lead score reaches a certain threshold, the CRM system automatically assigns the lead to a sales representative for personalized outreach.

Automating Social Media Lead Generation

Social media platforms offer powerful automation tools to help you reach a broader audience and capture leads more effectively. Social media automation includes scheduling posts, running ads, and using chatbots for engagement.

Tools for Social Media Automation:

- **Hootsuite and Buffer**: These platforms allow you to schedule posts, monitor engagement, and manage multiple social media accounts from a single dashboard.
- **Facebook and Instagram Ads**: Automated audience targeting and bidding features help optimize your ad campaigns for lead generation.
- **Social Media Chatbots**: Tools like ManyChat enable you to automate conversations with followers on

platforms like Facebook Messenger, capturing lead information or directing them to a landing page.

Example Workflow:

1. You schedule a series of promotional posts across social media platforms using Hootsuite.
2. A Facebook ad campaign targets specific audiences, driving traffic to a landing page.
3. A chatbot engages with visitors on your Facebook page, answers questions, and collects lead information.

Key Takeaway:

Automating lead generation and nurturing helps you capture more leads, engage them effectively, and guide them through the sales funnel without manual intervention. Automated tools streamline the process, ensuring that no lead is left behind and that prospects receive personalized, timely content.

3: Sales Automation for Scaling Offers

Automating Sales Workflows

Scaling your offer requires efficient sales processes that can handle increased demand without overwhelming your team. Sales automation streamlines repetitive tasks, allowing your sales team to focus on high-value activities such as closing deals and building relationships. Automation can handle tasks such as lead assignment, follow-ups, and pipeline management.

Key Automation Tools for Sales:

- **CRM Automation**: Tools like Salesforce, HubSpot CRM, and Pipedrive automatically capture leads, assign them to the appropriate sales reps, and track interactions throughout the sales pipeline.
- **Automated Follow-ups**: Platforms like Outreach.io and Yesware allow sales teams to automate follow-up emails and reminders, ensuring timely communication with prospects.
- **Sales Sequences**: Sales engagement platforms like SalesLoft allow you to create automated sales sequences that include a mix of emails, phone calls, and social media interactions, all tailored to each prospect's needs.

Example Workflow:

1. A lead is captured through a form on your website and automatically entered into your CRM.
2. Based on their lead score, the CRM assigns the lead to a sales representative and triggers a follow-up email.
3. The sales rep is notified to make a call after the lead has engaged with two emails from the automated sequence.

Automating the Sales Pipeline

Managing the sales pipeline manually becomes inefficient as your offer scales. Sales pipeline automation helps you track deals, forecast revenue, and manage tasks without losing track of where each lead or deal stands in the process.

Tools for Automating the Sales Pipeline:

- **Deal Tracking**: CRM systems like Salesforce and Pipedrive automatically update deal stages, assign tasks, and provide visual representations of your sales pipeline.
- **Task Automation**: Task management tools like Monday.com and Asana can be integrated with your CRM to automatically create tasks for sales reps based on deal stage or lead activity.
- **Automated Deal Notifications**: Receive notifications when deals move from one stage to the next or when a prospect takes a significant action, such as attending a demo or downloading a proposal.

Example Workflow:

1. A lead is added to the CRM, and a deal is automatically created.
2. The CRM tracks the lead's journey through the pipeline, moving them to the "Negotiation" stage after a sales call.
3. The system sends an automated notification to the sales rep when it's time to send a proposal or follow up.

Automating Quoting and Proposal Generation

As your offer scales, manually creating quotes and proposals for each prospect can become time-consuming and prone to errors. Automating this process helps streamline the sales cycle, reduce delays, and improve accuracy.

Tools for Automating Quotes and Proposals:

- **CPQ (Configure, Price, Quote) Software**: Tools like PandaDoc and Salesforce CPQ allow sales teams to automate the creation of quotes and proposals, complete with accurate pricing and contract terms.
- **eSignatures**: Platforms like DocuSign and HelloSign integrate with CPQ tools to automate contract generation and signing, speeding up the closing process.

Example Workflow:

1. A sales rep enters the deal's details into the CPQ system, which automatically generates a customized quote.
2. The quote is sent to the prospect, who can sign it electronically via DocuSign.
3. Once the contract is signed, the deal is automatically updated in the CRM, and the fulfillment team is notified to begin onboarding.

Key Takeaway:

Sales automation allows you to streamline the entire sales process, from lead assignment and follow-ups to pipeline management and proposal generation. By automating repetitive tasks, sales teams can focus on building relationships and closing deals, making it easier to scale your offer efficiently.

4: Marketing Automation for Scaling Offers

Automating Email Marketing Campaigns

Email marketing is one of the most effective channels for scaling an offer, but managing large-scale email campaigns manually can be time-consuming. Email marketing automation allows you to send personalized, targeted messages to your audience based on their behavior and preferences, ensuring that each recipient receives the right content at the right time.

Key Tools for Email Marketing Automation:

- **Mailchimp, ActiveCampaign, and HubSpot**: These platforms allow you to create automated email sequences, segment your audience based on behavior or demographics, and track performance metrics like open rates and conversions.
- **Behavioral Triggers**: Automated email platforms allow you to set up triggers based on customer actions, such as signing up for a webinar, downloading a resource, or abandoning a cart. These triggers ensure that the customer receives timely, relevant emails.
- **Personalization**: Dynamic content tools within email automation platforms enable you to personalize emails based on the recipient's name, preferences, location, or purchase history.

Example Workflow:

1. A customer adds an item to their cart but doesn't complete the purchase. This action triggers an

automated abandoned cart email reminding them to complete the purchase.

2. If the customer doesn't respond, a second email is automatically sent three days later, offering a limited-time discount.
3. Once the purchase is completed, the customer is added to a post-purchase email sequence that offers additional product recommendations.

Automating Social Media Marketing

Managing social media at scale requires consistent posting, audience engagement, and performance tracking. Social media automation tools allow you to schedule posts in advance, monitor engagement, and even respond to customer inquiries through chatbots.

Key Tools for Social Media Automation:

- **Buffer and Hootsuite**: These platforms allow you to schedule posts across multiple social media accounts, track engagement, and analyze performance metrics.
- **Social Media Ads Automation**: Facebook and Instagram Ads provide automated ad optimization features, such as dynamic ad targeting, retargeting, and automated bidding.
- **Chatbots**: Tools like ManyChat enable you to automate customer interactions on platforms like Facebook Messenger, providing instant responses to frequently asked questions or directing users to your website.

Example Workflow:

1. You schedule a month's worth of posts across Instagram, Facebook, and LinkedIn using Buffer.
2. An Instagram ad campaign is launched with automated bidding, dynamically targeting users based on their browsing behavior.
3. A chatbot on Facebook Messenger responds to user inquiries, provides product recommendations, and directs potential customers to your eCommerce store.

Automating Content Marketing

Content marketing plays a crucial role in attracting and educating your audience, but creating, publishing, and promoting content at scale can be overwhelming. Automating content workflows helps you stay consistent with content creation, promotion, and optimization.

Key Tools for Content Automation:

- **Content Calendars**: Tools like CoSchedule and Trello allow you to automate your content calendar, ensuring that blog posts, social media updates, and email campaigns are planned and published on time.
- **Content Distribution**: Platforms like Zapier can automate the distribution of your content across multiple channels, such as publishing a blog post and automatically sharing it on social media.
- **Content Optimization**: SEO tools like SEMrush and Ahrefs can automate keyword tracking, content

optimization, and backlink monitoring, helping you scale your content marketing efforts.

Example Workflow:

1. You create a blog post and schedule it in CoSchedule's content calendar for publication on your website.
2. Once the post is published, Zapier automatically shares it on your social media platforms and includes it in your next email newsletter.
3. SEMrush monitors the post's ranking and automatically suggests optimization opportunities based on keyword performance.

Automating Paid Advertising Campaigns

Paid advertising can generate immediate results when scaling an offer, but managing multiple ad campaigns across different platforms requires automation to ensure efficiency and performance. Advertising platforms like Google Ads and Facebook Ads offer powerful automation features that optimize targeting, bidding, and ad delivery.

Key Automation Features for Paid Advertising:

- **Automated Bidding**: Platforms like Google Ads and Facebook Ads use machine learning to adjust your bids automatically based on factors like time of day, audience behavior, and competition. This ensures that you get the best ROI without having to manually manage your bids.
- **Dynamic Ad Targeting**: Dynamic ads automatically personalize the ad content shown to users based on their browsing behavior or previous interactions with your brand.

- **Retargeting Ads**: Retargeting allows you to automatically display ads to users who have previously visited your website or engaged with your content. This keeps your brand top-of-mind and encourages users to return to complete a purchase.

Example Workflow:

1. A Google Ads campaign is launched with automated bidding, optimizing ad spend based on user behavior and competitive factors.
2. Facebook's dynamic ads feature personalizes product recommendations for each user based on their previous interactions with your website.
3. Retargeting ads are automatically displayed to users who visited your website but didn't convert, encouraging them to return and complete their purchase.

Key Takeaway:

Marketing automation is critical for scaling your offer across channels. From email and social media to content marketing and paid advertising, automation tools allow you to manage large-scale campaigns efficiently, deliver personalized experiences, and optimize performance in real time.

5: Automating Customer Service and Support

Automating Customer Support with Chatbots

Customer support is a crucial aspect of scaling an offer, especially as you begin serving a larger customer base. Automation tools like chatbots help you provide timely and effective support without overwhelming your team. Chatbots can handle common customer inquiries, provide product recommendations, and even assist with troubleshooting.

Key Tools for Automating Customer Support:

- **Intercom and Drift**: These platforms offer AI-powered chatbots that engage with customers in real-time, answering frequently asked questions, guiding users through the buying process, and escalating complex issues to a human agent.
- **Zendesk**: Zendesk's automation features include ticketing systems that route inquiries to the appropriate department, as well as self-service options like FAQs and knowledge bases.

Example Workflow:

1. A customer visits your website and engages with a chatbot to ask about shipping policies. The chatbot provides an instant response based on pre-programmed information.
2. If the inquiry is complex, the chatbot escalates the issue to a human agent, who is notified through the ticketing system.
3. After the issue is resolved, the chatbot follows up with the customer to ensure satisfaction.

Automating FAQs and Self-Service Options

Scaling customer service doesn't always require human interaction. Automating self-service options like FAQs, knowledge bases, and community forums allows customers to find answers to their questions without needing direct support from your team.

Tools for Automating Self-Service:

- **Help Scout and Freshdesk**: These platforms allow you to create automated FAQs, knowledge bases, and customer support articles, helping customers resolve issues on their own.
- **Community Forums**: Tools like Discourse and Vanilla Forums allow you to create online communities where customers can ask questions, share experiences, and provide support to one another.

Example Workflow:

1. A customer visits your website's knowledge base to find answers to their questions about using your product.
2. They use the search function to find a detailed how-to guide, resolving the issue without needing to contact customer support.
3. If they still need assistance, they can submit a ticket or contact a chatbot.

Automating Post-Purchase Support

Post-purchase support is essential for ensuring customer satisfaction and retention. Automating follow-up emails, surveys, and feedback requests helps you stay connected with customers after they've made a purchase, while also collecting valuable insights for improvement.

Tools for Automating Post-Purchase Support:

- **Klaviyo and ActiveCampaign**: These email automation platforms allow you to set up automated post-purchase email sequences that include product instructions, usage tips, and requests for reviews or feedback.
- **SurveyMonkey**: Automate customer satisfaction surveys to gather feedback after a purchase or customer service interaction.

Example Workflow:

- After a customer makes a purchase, they receive an automated email with product usage tips and a request to leave a review.
- One week later, a follow-up email is sent, asking the customer to complete a satisfaction survey.
- Based on the customer's feedback, the system automatically segments them into a loyalty program or offers additional support if needed.

Key Takeaway:

Automating customer service and support allows you to handle a larger volume of inquiries while maintaining a high level of service. Chatbots, self-service options, and post-purchase automation ensure that customers receive timely, accurate assistance without overwhelming your support team.

6: Operational Automation for Scaling Offers

Automating Order Fulfillment and Inventory Management

As your offer scales, managing order fulfillment and inventory becomes increasingly complex. Automating these processes helps you keep track of stock levels, manage shipping, and ensure timely delivery without the need for manual intervention.

Key Tools for Automating Fulfillment and Inventory:

- **ShipBob and ShipStation**: These platforms automate order fulfillment, allowing you to streamline the shipping process, track orders in real-time, and integrate with your eCommerce platform.
- **Shopify and WooCommerce**: Both platforms offer automation features that sync your sales, inventory, and fulfillment processes, ensuring that stock levels are updated automatically as orders are placed.
- **Inventory Management Software**: Tools like TradeGecko and Cin7 automate inventory tracking, ensuring that you never run out of stock or over-order.

Example Workflow:

1. A customer places an order through your eCommerce store, which is automatically synced with your fulfillment platform (e.g., ShipBob).
2. The platform manages the entire shipping process, from picking and packing to tracking the delivery.

3. Once the order is shipped, the customer receives an automated notification with tracking details.

Automating Billing and Payments

Billing and payments can be a significant source of friction as you scale your offer. Automating the invoicing, payment collection, and subscription management processes helps ensure timely payments while reducing the risk of errors.

Key Tools for Automating Billing and Payments:

- **Stripe and PayPal**: These platforms offer automated billing and payment solutions, including recurring billing for subscription-based offers, payment notifications, and dispute resolution.
- **Xero and QuickBooks**: Accounting software like Xero and QuickBooks automates invoicing, expense tracking, and payment reconciliation, ensuring that your financial processes are efficient and error-free.
- **Chargebee and Recurly**: These platforms automate subscription billing, allowing you to manage recurring payments, upgrade/downgrade options, and customer retention efforts.

Example Workflow:

1. A customer signs up for a monthly subscription to your service through Stripe.
2. Stripe automatically charges the customer's payment method each month and sends a receipt via email.

3. If the payment fails, the system automatically retries the payment or sends a notification to the customer.

Automating Reporting and Analytics

As your offer scales, tracking performance across sales, marketing, and operations becomes more complex. Automating your reporting and analytics processes ensures that you have real-time visibility into key metrics without needing to manually compile data from different sources.

Key Tools for Automating Reporting:

- **Google Analytics and Data Studio**: Google Analytics provides automated tracking of website traffic, conversions, and user behavior. Data Studio allows you to create custom dashboards that automatically pull data from multiple sources.
- **Tableau and Power BI**: These business intelligence tools provide advanced analytics and reporting features, allowing you to automate data visualization and generate real-time reports.

Example Workflow:

1. Google Analytics tracks your website traffic and conversion rates, while your CRM tracks sales and customer interactions.
2. Data from both systems is automatically pulled into a custom dashboard in Google Data Studio, providing real-time insights into your marketing and sales performance.
3. The dashboard is automatically updated daily, allowing you to monitor key metrics like conversion

rate, customer acquisition cost (CAC), and customer lifetime value (LTV) without manual effort.

Key Takeaway:

Operational automation streamlines essential processes like order fulfillment, billing, and reporting, allowing your business to scale efficiently. By automating these back-end operations, you can ensure that your offer is delivered consistently, payments are processed on time, and performance is monitored accurately.

Conclusion: Leveraging Automation to Scale Offers Efficiently

Scaling an offer successfully requires more than just attracting more customers—it demands efficient systems, consistent communication, and streamlined operations to handle increased demand without compromising on quality or customer experience. Automation provides the tools needed to achieve these goals, allowing businesses to scale their offers while maintaining efficiency and profitability.

Final Key Takeaways:

1. **Automate Lead Generation and Nurturing**: Use automation tools to capture and nurture leads, ensuring that prospects receive personalized, timely content throughout the customer journey.
2. **Streamline Sales Processes**: Sales automation enables your team to manage more leads and close more deals without manual effort. Automate

follow-ups, lead scoring, and pipeline management to improve efficiency.

3. **Scale Marketing Efforts**: Marketing automation across email, social media, content marketing, and paid advertising helps you reach a larger audience, deliver personalized experiences, and optimize performance in real time.
4. **Enhance Customer Service**: Automate customer support with chatbots, self-service options, and post-purchase communication to handle a growing volume of inquiries without overwhelming your team.
5. **Optimize Operations**: Automate back-end processes like order fulfillment, billing, and reporting to ensure that your offer is delivered consistently and efficiently as your business scales.

Looking Ahead

As you continue to scale your offer, automation will play an increasingly important role in ensuring your business remains agile, efficient, and responsive to customer needs. By leveraging the right automation tools and strategies, you can continue growing your business while maintaining a high level of service and operational excellence.

Automation is not just a tool for efficiency—it's a critical component of scaling offers sustainably and profitably. With the right systems in place, businesses can expand their reach, increase conversions, and ultimately dominate their markets with compelling, scalable offers.

Chapter 19

CRAFTING OFFERS FOR SERVICE-BASED BUSINESSES

Service-based businesses face unique challenges and opportunities when it comes to creating compelling offers. Unlike product-based businesses, which rely on tangible goods, service providers sell intangible value, making it essential to communicate benefits clearly, establish trust, and deliver a sense of reliability. Crafting an irresistible offer for a service-based business involves presenting not only the service itself but also the outcomes, the experience, and the expertise behind the service.

We'll cover key components of effective offers, ways to differentiate yourself in the marketplace, how to structure your service packages, and how to use bonuses, guarantees, and pricing strategies to make your offer irresistible.

1: Understanding the Service-Based Business Model

The Nature of Service-Based Offers

Service-based businesses, unlike product-based companies, focus on delivering value through expertise, time, skills, or specialized knowledge. Because services are intangible, potential customers can't "test" or "hold" what you're offering before they purchase. This makes the process of creating and delivering offers much more reliant on trust, reputation, and clearly defined value propositions.

Examples of service-based businesses include:

- Consulting firms
- Coaching or mentorship programs
- Agencies (marketing, PR, design, etc.)
- Legal services
- Medical or healthcare services
- Home services (plumbing, electrical, cleaning)

The Importance of a Strong Offer in Service-Based Businesses

Creating a compelling offer is critical for service-based businesses because it helps potential clients understand the specific value they will receive, making it easier for them to justify the purchase. A well-crafted offer can:

- Highlight the benefits and outcomes of the service.
- Differentiate your business from competitors by focusing on unique selling points (USPs).
- Overcome objections by addressing common concerns (e.g., time, cost, results).
- Provide clarity on what the client can expect in terms of deliverables, timelines, and ROI.

Challenges in Crafting Service-Based Offers

Service-based businesses face unique challenges when developing offers, including:

1. **Intangibility:** It can be difficult to explain the value of an intangible service, especially if the results are long-term or subjective (such as consulting or coaching).
2. **Customization:** Many services are customized based on client needs, making it harder to create standardized packages or pricing models.
3. **Trust and Credibility:** Clients need to trust your expertise and experience before they commit to purchasing a service, which is often a high-ticket investment.

Key Takeaway:

In a service-based business, crafting a compelling offer requires focusing on the outcomes and benefits your clients will experience, building trust, and clearly communicating your expertise. A strong offer helps differentiate your services from competitors and creates confidence in potential clients that you can deliver results.

2: Key Components of a Service-Based Offer

1. Value Proposition

A strong value proposition is the foundation of any compelling offer. In service-based businesses, the value proposition should clearly explain what your clients will gain from working with you. This involves understanding the key problems your target market faces and positioning your service as the solution.

How to Craft a Service-Based Value Proposition:

- **Identify the Pain Points:** What are the common challenges or issues your clients are facing that your service can solve?
- **Communicate the Benefits:** Instead of focusing solely on the service itself, highlight the outcomes or benefits. For example, if you run a marketing agency, your value proposition could emphasize "increasing lead generation by 30% within three months" rather than just offering "digital marketing services."
- **Focus on Transformation:** Especially in high-ticket services, clients want to know how your service will transform their business or life. Paint a picture of the before-and-after scenario.

Example:

If you run a business coaching service, your value proposition could be: "I help entrepreneurs double their revenue in six months by implementing proven business strategies."

2. Unique Selling Proposition (USP)

Your USP sets you apart from competitors and gives potential clients a clear reason to choose you over others. For service-based businesses, your USP might include your specialized expertise, your unique process, or your personal approach to delivering results.

How to Identify Your USP:

- **Niche Expertise:** Are you an expert in a specific industry or service? Highlight your depth of knowledge in that area.

- **Proprietary Processes:** Do you have a unique system, framework, or method that delivers superior results?
- **Personalized Service:** Can you offer a more customized or hands-on experience compared to your competitors?
- **Client Success Stories:** Can you demonstrate better results through testimonials, case studies, or success stories?

Example:

A fitness trainer could have a USP like, "I specialize in helping busy professionals lose weight through short, effective workouts that fit into any schedule."

3. Service Deliverables

Service deliverables clearly define what the client will receive when they purchase your service. This is crucial for managing expectations and building trust.

Key Elements of Service Deliverables:

- Scope of Work: Define what tasks or activities are included in your service. For example, if you offer social media management, you might specify that the deliverables include posting three times per week, engaging with followers, and creating monthly reports.
- Timelines: Include a clear timeline for when clients can expect to see results or receive deliverables. This helps manage expectations and reassures clients about the value of your service.

- Communication Plan: Specify how and when clients will hear from you. Will you have weekly check-ins? Will they receive a report at the end of the project? Clear communication reduces client anxiety and creates transparency.

Example:

For a web design service, deliverables might include a customized website with up to five pages, a responsive design, SEO optimization, and one round of revisions, all delivered within six weeks.

4. Outcome-Focused Messaging

One of the most important aspects of crafting an offer for a service-based business is focusing on the outcomes, not just the **process. Clients don't** care as much about the technical details of what you do; they care about the results you will deliver.

How to Create Outcome-Focused Messaging:

- Highlight Tangible Results: Use specific, quantifiable results when possible. For example, "We help businesses increase their website traffic by 50% within three months."
- Use Client Success Stories: Share real-world examples of clients who have achieved success using your services. Case studies and testimonials are powerful ways to demonstrate outcomes.
- Future-Proofing: Focus on how your service will provide lasting value. For example, "We'll build a customized SEO strategy that continues to drive traffic for years to come."

Example:

Instead of saying, "I offer bookkeeping services," you could say, "I'll streamline your bookkeeping processes, so you save 10 hours a week and can focus on growing your business."

Key Takeaway:

Service-based offers should emphasize the value clients will receive, the uniqueness of your service, the specific deliverables included, and the outcomes they can expect. By focusing on these core components, you can create offers that speak directly to the needs and desires of your target market.

3: Structuring Service Packages

Why Service Packages Are Important

Service packages allow you to offer your clients different tiers of service at varying price points. This helps accommodate different budgets and needs, allowing clients to choose the level of service that works best for them. Packaging your services also makes your offer more tangible, helping clients understand exactly what they are getting.

Types of Service Packages

There are several ways to structure your service packages, depending on your business model and the needs of your clients.

1. Tiered Packages

Tiered packages offer different levels of service, often categorized as basic, standard, and premium. Each level includes more features or services, allowing clients to choose the package that fits their needs.

Example: Social Media Management

- **Basic Package:** Posting three times per week, basic engagement, and monthly reporting.
- **Standard Package:** Posting five times per week, advanced engagement (including DMs), bi-weekly reports, and basic ad management.
- **Premium Package:** Daily posting, full engagement, weekly reports, ad management, and strategy sessions.

Benefits of Tiered Packages:

- Increased flexibility: Clients can choose a package that fits their budget.
- Upsell opportunities: You can easily upsell clients to a higher-tier package as they grow or see results.
- Clear comparison: Showing different levels of service makes it easier for clients to compare and understand the value of higher-tier packages.

2. Customizable Packages

Customizable packages allow clients to choose from a list of services or add-ons to create a tailored solution. This is ideal for service-based businesses that offer highly personalized services.

Example: Digital Marketing Agency

You could offer a base package (e.g., SEO, email marketing, social media management) and let clients add additional services like paid advertising or content creation based on their needs.

Benefits of Customizable Packages:

- **Personalization:** Clients feel that they're getting exactly what they need, which increases satisfaction.
- **Flexible pricing:** You can adjust pricing based on the scope of services chosen.
- **Tailored solutions:** This is especially effective for businesses where every client's needs are different.

3. Retainer Packages

For businesses that offer ongoing services (such as consulting, coaching, or digital marketing), retainer packages provide a consistent income stream while allowing clients to access your services on an ongoing basis.

Example: Consulting Service

A consultant might offer monthly retainer packages where clients receive a certain number of consulting hours per month, as well as access to additional resources or support.

Benefits of Retainer Packages:

- **Steady income:** Retainers provide a predictable and consistent revenue stream.
- **Client loyalty:** Ongoing services help build long-term relationships with clients.

- **Scalable:** You can offer additional services or hours as clients' needs grow.

Pricing Service Packages

Pricing is a critical aspect of crafting service packages. You want to price your packages in a way that reflects the value you deliver while being accessible to your target audience.

Key Considerations for Pricing:

- **Cost of delivery:** Calculate the time, effort, and resources required to deliver the service. Ensure your pricing covers these costs while leaving room for a profit margin.
- **Competitor analysis:** Research competitors to understand industry pricing standards. However, don't simply price-match—focus on the value you bring to justify premium pricing if needed.
- **Perceived value:** Your pricing should reflect the perceived value of your service. Higher prices often convey greater expertise or higher quality, so don't undervalue your services out of fear of losing clients.

Psychological Pricing Strategies:

- **Charm pricing:** Pricing a package at $997 instead of $1,000 can make the price seem more affordable, even though the difference is minimal.
- **Anchoring:** Offer a high-priced premium package to make your mid-tier package seem more affordable and valuable by comparison.

Key Takeaway:

Structuring service packages allows you to offer flexibility, tailor services to client needs, and maximize revenue through tiered pricing, customizable options, or retainers. Focus on delivering clear value at every pricing tier to ensure clients understand the benefits of each package.

4: Using Bonuses and Guarantees to Make Your Offer Irresistible

Adding Bonuses to Enhance Your Offer

Bonuses are additional services or resources that you include with your offer to increase its perceived value. Offering bonuses can make your service package more appealing by providing extra value that clients didn't expect.

Examples of Effective Bonuses:

- **Additional consulting sessions:** For clients who sign up for your premium package, offer an extra hour of consulting per month at no additional cost.
- **Exclusive resources:** Provide access to a library of eBooks, templates, or checklists that clients can use to improve their own processes.
- **Priority support:** Offer faster response times or priority access to your support team for higher-tier packages.

Benefits of Bonuses:

- **Increases perceived value:** Clients feel they are getting more than they paid for, making the decision to purchase easier.

- **Differentiates your offer:** Bonuses can set your offer apart from competitors by providing added benefits they don't offer.
- **Encourages upsells:** You can tie bonuses to higher-tier packages, encouraging clients to choose more expensive options to get the extra benefits.

Implementing Guarantees to Reduce Risk

One of the main barriers to purchasing a service is the perceived risk. Clients worry about whether they'll see the promised results or if they'll waste their investment. Offering guarantees helps reduce this perceived risk and provides reassurance that you stand behind your services.

Types of Guarantees for Service-Based Offers:

- **Money-back guarantee:** Offer a satisfaction guarantee, where clients can get a refund if they don't see results within a certain time frame.
- **Results-based guarantee:** Promise a specific result or outcome, such as "We'll increase your website traffic by 20% within 90 days, or you don't pay."
- **Risk-free trial:** Offer a free trial of your service (e.g., a complimentary consultation or access to your service for 30 days) to allow clients to experience the benefits before committing fully.

Benefits of Guarantees:

- **Builds trust:** Guarantees show clients that you're confident in your ability to deliver results.

- **Reduces buyer hesitation:** Offering a guarantee removes the fear of wasting money, making it easier for clients to say "yes" to your offer.
- **Increases conversions:** By reducing the perceived risk, guarantees can significantly boost your conversion rates.

Key Takeaway:

Adding bonuses and guarantees to your service offer increases its perceived value and reduces the risk for clients, making it easier for them to commit. By offering extras and standing behind your service with guarantees, you build trust and create an irresistible offer that clients feel confident investing in.

5: Pricing Strategies for Service-Based Offers

Value-Based Pricing

In service-based businesses, pricing should be based on the value you deliver to clients rather than the time or effort you invest. Value-based pricing focuses on the outcomes and transformations you provide, allowing you to charge higher rates when the perceived value is high.

How to Implement Value-Based Pricing:

- **Understand the client's goals:** What results does the client expect from your service, and how valuable are those results to their business or life?
- **Price according to outcomes:** If you help a business generate an additional $100,000 in

revenue through your marketing services, your pricing should reflect the magnitude of that outcome.

- **Communicate the ROI:** Use your offer to clearly explain the return on investment (ROI) that clients can expect from your services. For example, "By investing $5,000 in our SEO services, you can expect to generate $50,000 in additional revenue over the next 12 months."

Tiered Pricing Strategy

Offering multiple pricing tiers gives clients flexibility in choosing the level of service that best fits their needs and budget. Tiered pricing also creates an opportunity for upselling, as clients may start with a lower-tier package and upgrade as they see results.

Example of Tiered Pricing:

- **Basic Package:** $1,000/month for SEO services targeting 10 keywords.
- **Standard Package:** $2,000/month for SEO services targeting 20 keywords, plus monthly reporting.
- **Premium Package:** $3,500/month for SEO services targeting 30 keywords, reporting, and bi-weekly strategy sessions.

Premium Pricing Strategy

Premium pricing involves positioning your services as high-value and charging accordingly. This strategy works well for businesses that offer highly specialized or niche services and can deliver exceptional results. Premium pricing often includes more personalized service, faster turnaround times, and exclusive bonuses.

How to Implement Premium Pricing:

- **Position yourself as an expert:** Establish your authority in your niche through content marketing, speaking engagements, and client success stories.
- **Create exclusivity:** Limit the number of clients you take on, or offer VIP packages that come with personalized attention and priority service.
- **Use premium branding:** Ensure your branding, website, and marketing materials reflect the high-end nature of your services.

Key Takeaway:

Pricing strategies for service-based businesses should be focused on the value and outcomes you deliver to clients. Whether you use value-based, tiered, or premium pricing, ensure that your prices reflect the transformation clients can expect from your services.

Conclusion: Creating Compelling Offers for Service-Based Businesses

Crafting an offer for a service-based business requires a deep understanding of your clients' needs and desires, clear communication of the outcomes you deliver, and a strong focus on building trust. By incorporating a compelling value proposition, a unique selling proposition, and clear service deliverables, you can create offers that resonate with potential clients and encourage them to take action.

Final Key Takeaways:

1. **Focus on the Outcomes:** Clients want to know what they'll gain from your service, so emphasize the results and transformations you provide.
2. **Differentiate with Your USP:** Highlight what makes your service unique, whether it's your expertise, personalized approach, or proprietary processes.
3. **Use Bonuses and Guarantees:** Adding extra value through bonuses and reducing risk through guarantees can significantly increase the appeal of your offer.
4. **Tailor Your Pricing Strategy:** Use value-based, tiered, or premium pricing to ensure your services are accessible to a range of clients while reflecting the value you deliver.

By applying these principles, you'll be able to craft service-based offers that not only attract clients but also position your business for long-term success. A well-crafted offer builds trust, clearly communicates value, and creates a seamless path for clients to choose your services over the competition.

CONCLUSION: YOU ARE SOLD! BY ROHIT SONI

In today's highly competitive marketplace, the ability to create irresistible offers is a powerful skill that can set your business apart and drive success. Whether you're selling products, services, or digital solutions, the effectiveness of your offer is a determining factor in attracting and converting customers. Throughout this book, we've explored the key principles, strategies, and techniques for crafting offers that not only capture attention but also compel action. Now, it's time to reflect on the core lessons and how you can apply them to dominate your market with irresistible offers.

The Core Components of an Irresistible Offer

At the heart of any successful offer lies a combination of factors that, when executed well, make it impossible for customers to say "no." These Include a compelling value proposition, a deep understanding of your target audience, and an offer structure that minimizes risk while maximizing perceived value.

The foundation of any offer is your **value proposition**—the promise of specific benefits and results that your customer will gain. The key to an irresistible offer is not just telling customers about your product or service but making them feel like they *need* it. This is achieved by clearly articulating how your offer solves their pain points, fulfills their desires, or helps them achieve their goals. Throughout the book, we've emphasized the importance of focusing on **outcomes over features**—customers care more about the results they'll experience than the technical details of what you provide.

You also need to deeply understand your **target audience**—what motivates them, what frustrates them, and what they value most. This understanding allows you to tailor your offer to their specific needs, making it more relevant and personalized. The best offers speak directly to the heart of the customer's problems and provide clear solutions that are easy to grasp and emotionally resonant.

In addition to understanding your audience, your offer needs to minimize perceived risk and maximize perceived value. This is where elements like **risk reversal**, **guarantees**, and **bonuses** come into play. Offering a money-back guarantee, for instance, can significantly reduce the hesitation a customer might feel. Similarly, adding valuable bonuses can increase the perceived worth of your offer, tipping the scales in your favor.

Key Offer-Making Strategies to Implement

As we've discussed throughout the book, crafting an irresistible offer involves combining a set of well-honed strategies. Here are some of the most important strategies you should focus on as you continue to refine and scale your offers:

1. **Leverage Scarcity and Urgency**: Scarcity (limited availability) and urgency (time-sensitive offers) are psychological triggers that create a sense of fear of missing out (FOMO). Whether it's offering limited-time discounts or exclusive bonuses to the first 100 customers, these techniques can push customers to take action sooner rather than later.
2. **Use Social Proof**: People trust what others have already endorsed. Customer testimonials, case studies, and reviews add a level of credibility and trust to your offer. When potential buyers see that others have had positive experiences, they're more likely to feel confident about their purchase decision.
3. **Bundle and Add Bonuses**: Customers love getting more for their money, and adding bonuses or bundling complementary products or services together is an excellent way to increase the perceived value of your offer. Ensure that the bonuses align with the main product or service and provide additional utility or benefit to the customer.
4. **Implement a Clear Call-to-Action (CTA)**: Your offer should leave no doubt about what the next step is. A strong, clear call-to-action tells your customers exactly what to do and why they should do it now. Whether it's "Buy Now," "Get Started," or "Claim Your Free Trial," a well-placed CTA can make all the difference in converting leads into customers.
5. **Test and Optimize**: One of the key themes discussed in this book is the importance of

continuously testing and optimizing your offers. Markets shift, customer preferences evolve, and what works today may not work tomorrow. A/B testing different elements of your offer—such as headlines, pricing, and bonuses—helps you determine what resonates most with your audience. Optimization is not a one-time event but an ongoing process that will ensure your offers remain competitive and effective over time.

Turning Knowledge into Action: The Path Forward

Now that you've gained insight into the fundamental principles of creating irresistible offers, the next step is to put that knowledge into action. It's not enough to understand the concepts—you need to experiment, refine, and iterate to see what works best for your business and your audience.

Start with a Single Offer

Choose one offer to focus on first. This could be your core product or service, or it could be a promotional offer you're preparing to launch. Start by revisiting the key elements discussed in this book:

- Is your value proposition clear and compelling?
- Does your offer address your audience's pain points and deliver real benefits?
- Are you leveraging social proof, scarcity, or urgency to drive action?

Once you've developed this offer, test it in the market. Gather feedback, track conversion rates, and identify areas for improvement.

Build on Success

As you gain traction with your first offer, build on that success by expanding or refining your offers.

Automate and Scale

Once you have a winning offer, look for ways to automate and scale it. Whether through email marketing, retargeting campaigns, or sales funnels, automation allows you to reach a larger audience and maintain consistent marketing efforts without constantly needing to start from scratch.

Final Thoughts: The Power of Irresistible Offers

Creating an irresistible offer is not just about selling a product or service—it's about offering value, building trust, and establishing a connection with your customers. It's about positioning your business as the obvious choice in a crowded marketplace by demonstrating that you understand your customers' needs and can deliver results.

The strategies outlined in this book provide a comprehensive framework for crafting offers that are designed to convert. Whether you're just starting out or looking to refine your approach, mastering the art of creating irresistible offers will open new doors for your business and allow you to achieve sustainable growth.

As you continue on your journey, remember that the best offers evolve over time. Stay attuned to your audience's changing needs, remain flexible in your approach, and keep testing and optimizing your offers. With persistence and creativity, you'll be well on your way to building offers that not only drive sales but also foster long-term customer loyalty.

Here's to your success in mastering the art of irresistible offers and taking your business to new heights!

SOME OF AUTHOR'S BIGGEST SUCCESS STORIES

Client Success Story

"Rohit has worked for me over the last few months and have completely changed around my social media game. Amplify Media is solely been responsible for increased income, increase profits, increased happiness and joy in my life. Thanks Rohit for what you have done for me."

– Ken D Foster (Business Strategist, Life Coach, Best Selling Author)

"For anyone considering hiring Rohit, he has worked for me to create some masterclasses he did one a month ago we got 129 people registered and made over $100K with the offers, copy and his email. So if you're someone looking to up their social media marketing game. I highly recommend Rohit."

– Terrance Mcmahon (Financial Advisor, Business Coach, TEDx Speaker)

'I am Rosa Rodriguez I am a business coach, I was blown away by how much effort Rohit and his company Amplify Media put in creating my social media messaging and since I have started working with them, I have already got my first 5-FIGURE day not only that I have been able to stay consistent with my content, so if you're a business who is really busy and want to add more clients, contact Rohit Soni."

– Rosa Rodriguez (Money and Mindset Coach)

Thankyou from the bottom of my heart for reading, grabbing knowledge, making notes and most importantly implementing the strategies that I have shared.

You see it took me over 4 years, constant rejections, failures to get to where I am in the marketing world.

I am not PERFECT, but I know what works and what doesn't. So this book is a guide for you to start getting results because offers is what sets your product/service apart. Just getting your offer right will help you scale your business in more ways than one.

So THANKS again for reading this book.

www.ingramcontent.com/pod-product-compliance
Lightning Source LLC
LaVergne TN
LVHW091253150826
845673LV00006B/1403